AF372219

Dedication:

I would like to dedicate this to all of the therapists out there. To my two ladies, A. and K, you are my saviors and will always be part of my heart.
Also, Y.S. You are more amazing than you know.

Thank you to all of my friends and family that supported me in this journey. Especially S.W.S. you are a true gift. Thank you for going above and beyond in our friendship.

All of your continued advice, kind words, and encouragement mean the world to me.

Evie Su Joy

From...,

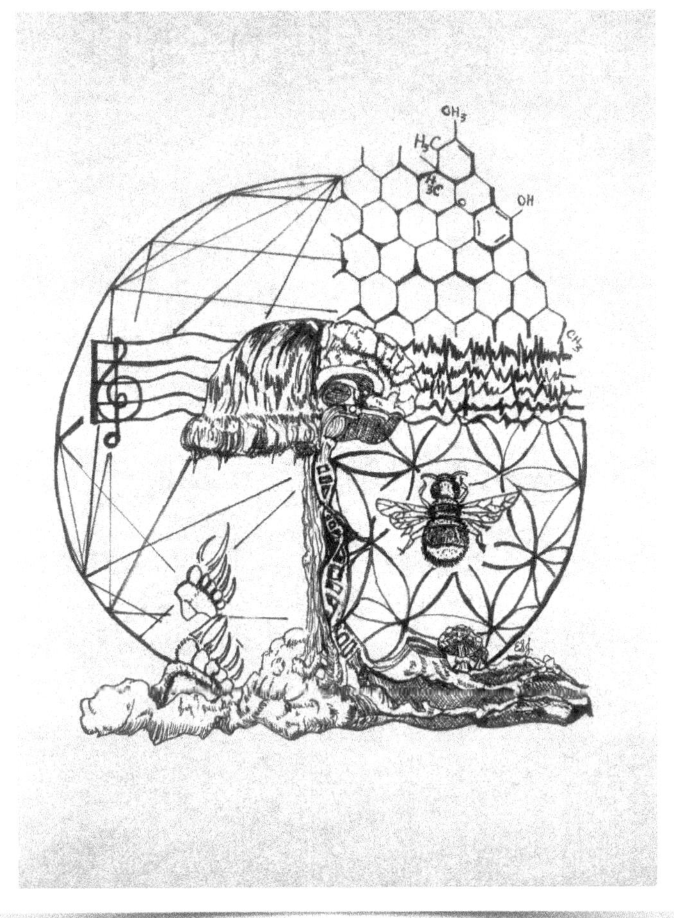

To...,

My Journey of Learning To BE

Table Of Contents

Introduction

Life had become like a void. Depression was ruling my mind. I was drifting. I was always sad. Even with medication I just couldn't get my mind where I wanted it to be. I wanted to leave this Earth. I knew that the time had come to move myself forward. I knew I couldn't live in the mindset that had me in survival mode. I accidentally found a program that changed everything.

The program that I reference in my story was the catalyst to my awakening. I had come to the limits of my medication's help. There was obviously more to do or I wouldn't have been struggling and continuously fighting depression and its many symptoms.

There are many paths that lead to what we know as ascension. My path involved TV, movies, music, books, and of course the internet. The "usual" path is by spending countless hours learning how to meditate and finding some higher spiritual path.

I found mine in a very unique way. Religion played absolutely NO part in this awakening. It goes to show that there is more out there that we don't know nor understand.

If this journey of mine helps another to find their path in their own unconventional way, then maybe they can help another.

I hope my story brings those that are curious and searching closer and more accepting of themselves. My love for myself grows every day. I hope I can encourage my readers to learn to love themselves and their life.

The process for me to awaken lasted over six months. I wrote and journaled as it was happening. My story starts at that point where I question everything and my purpose in this world.

CHAPTER 1

FROM "I WAS," TO "I AM"

For most people, there comes a time when we realize that we aren't living the life that we imagined as a child. We envisioned fame and fortune, peace and prosperity, adventure and comfort. Rarely, do we as humans, get to actually fulfill those imaginings of our childhoods.

We watch as what seems like a fortunate few get their dream lives. Our natural and human response is usually jealousy. It is an easy emotion. But, it does nothing but negatively impact our psyche. We walk around not mentally developed enough to understand what may be required to reach those heights of our existence. Most aren't even aware of what it will take to reach that "dream life."

Sometimes it baffles me how others live their lives without ever leaving that lower level of human comprehension and evolution. What drives them? How many of them are just pushing their way through their life? How many hate their life? And, why? What is the default human experience?

Most people either don't know where to start or what can even be done to improve themselves. Issues like stress, and lack of energy or motivation can become somewhat of a crutch or an excuse that we use to mask our fear of the unknown. (I am not talking about those with medical conditions.)

We need to examine our life. Not just where we may currently be. We need to look as far back as we can. We need to see every emotion, even if we are confused by them or traumatized in some way by them. What ever caused that lasting scar... that must be softened. It must be examined from all sides before we can understand its reach and impact on our life.

I have learned why my life brings me such confusion and fear. And, I now know why I have that ever present sense of doom or that something will go wrong. It all stems from the fact that I grew up in a home with an emotionally and physically abusive narcissist mother and an enabling neglectful father. Of course, This is not a diagnoses that she got from her doctor because she hasn't seen a doctor. As most narcissist do, she thinks nothing is wrong with her or her actions.

No, my therapists and psychiatrist informed me of the signs and gave me their professional viewpoint. They know all of the signs.

There seems to be a great number of narcissist parents out there for the now grown children from my generation. I have learned so much about the characters that a narcissist parent will assign to the people in their lives. There is the "Golden Child," the "Scapegoat," and the "Neutral Child." In the studies of narcissists, I became aware that I was assigned the role known as the "scapegoat."

I know this from many self help books and years of therapy.

Therapy was not something that was commonplace in my upbringing. It took me a while to not only hit rock bottom, but want to improve so much that I had to trust a stranger with my darkness.

I didn't settle for the first therapist that I visited. It didn't feel right and the whole energy felt off. My second visit, (after calling around to get appointments) I found Alyssa. Therapy has changed my life in so many ways. Most are positive.

Actually, the only down side is that my wonderful therapist, Alyssa, retired and is now traveling the world with her future husband. I want to be jealous, but she is so wonderful, I can't help but be happy for her. But, that left me without her and a need to start over in therapy, history wise, with a new therapist. Alyssa left some big shoes.

But, just having someone listen to me, that is not connected in any way to my family, and then validating everything I said, was an unexplainable gift. Everyone I had previously shared my troubles with knew my mother and father and knew their status in the community. There was the feeling that nothing could be done.

Mothers!

Why does it always seem to come back to

mothers? It seems that the previous generations who lived in the more restrictive time for women used their children as their mode of release. The life or actions that would have been meant for the world were put on the children of these women.

My Mother was/is like a viper. She is like a "snake" that slithers her way into someone's life and whispers threats that no one else can hear or would even believe came out of her mouth.

She always had a way of inserting her venom into every aspect of my life. All of my friends and ANY adult that showed me favor or even kindness, she made a point of killing those connections as best she could or she would at least insert herself in every conversation or situation if possible. She made a point of connecting with anyone I was connected with on social media too. I recently deleted those apps and have enjoyed the freedom.

But, her impact is the main source of the delay in my personal growth and a big part of why I don't know who I am meant to be to this world. She is a HUGE part of my memory. Not

all are bad memories, either. She did just
enough mothering to lure me in and then
would remind me of my place in her existence.
I was secondary to her goals. It was never her
intention to be the mother I needed. She
wouldn't have known what I needed anyway,
because she never took the time to get to
know her own children. I have one older sister,
two younger brothers and a younger sister. I
am the second of five children; the true middle
child. We were just reflections of and to her.
Our lives were hers to manipulate and ruin. If
she ever struggled in her evil intent, to be kind
to us, I never saw it. She never held back her
rage. She did however struggle to put on a
"kind face" of the loving mom in public though.
So, I know what it looked like.

There were a couple of times, I got the "MOM"
I always wanted. The first time was when I had
my first baby. She came out to New Mexico for
the birth. I was in the United States Air Force
(USAF) at the time. My oldest son was born at
the civilian hospital there. My mom decided
that it would be "best" if she came out with
my Mother-in-law, for her third grandchild's
birth. It was my Mother's-in-law first grand-
baby. Of course, it was all for appearances. I

knew it. But I wasn't expecting her to pull up all of her deeply hidden mothering instincts. She was being watched by everyone. She really put on a show. I reveled in it…soaked it up. I knew her mood or personality could shift wildly if she was ever left alone with me. She wasn't… and so it didn't. When she left, I actually cried. Never have I ever wanted her to stay for a while longer like then.

As long as my Mother-in-law stayed too, that is. Had she not been there, I know things would have been different. Without a witness to my mother's kindness, I know her facade would have slipped a time or two, if she would have even visited at all. I actually can't recall another time where she presented herself so loving. She was the picture perfect mom of the new mother that most long for after having a baby.

The next time she got close, was when my youngest son graduated from high school and she came to visit my new home.

My husband and I had recently bought our very first home in a tiny town on the Eastern Shore of Maryland. A mid 1800's GORGEOUS

Victorian styled home that needed (and still needs) some love. But, it is over 5300 square feet, three stories (plus a cellar) and gorgeous! The kitchen is a dream come true... the whole house is, really. We are in love with it and hope we can stay here for a long while.

Having this gorgeous home somehow brought out a very loving side to my mom. She now calls me, "Sweet Girl!" Why? I cannot figure out her end game. Maybe because I only know what it feels like to be a victim of her game.

I know that she somehow thinks that what I have reflects onto her. Up until we got this home, she stayed the same toward me. I have brothers and sisters who all achieved the goal of having their own home years ago. All four of my siblings seemed to build within a 10-year span. We couldn't because we were poor. When I say poor, I mean it.

Just to put it into perspective, my husband took a 52% pay-cut when he got out of the Army. My family of five survived somehow on less than $25,000 a year for four years. All of the kids were in school at the time, too. Now, we had been poor before but had hoped that each time would be the last. We have been on WIC, food stamps, and anything else we could qualify for. It had only been semi-good for us in the later years of my husband's Army service. Being poor is hard on kids, but they learned great lessons about life.

My mom didn't seem to care so much when we suffered, even when we lived less then five miles from her home that last time we "struck it poor." Even though she would tell us that we needed to move "home," and that they would help us, I am assuming that she meant my in-laws. She never offered help in any way, shape, or form, and man, did we need it. Luckily, my husband's family has always been there when we really needed them.

I have lived in a few states besides my home state of Mississippi in my nearly three-decade marriage. My mom has only visited me six times in 30 years! Two of those times happened in the four years we lived close. She only came to my house to visit without being officially invited for a birthday or holiday event, two times. Two!

But now, after we bought our first home, she

wanted to visit me again. Or maybe she just wanted a chance to be alone with me in my dream house so she could remind me that she was much younger when she bought her first house... or maybe she would tell me how to decorate this house differently. I already know that she would make this place a showstopper at Christmas. How do I know? Well, she told me when she visited for my son's graduation, of course.

She made sure to point out that it would take me years to build up to her level of showboating-ness. I wouldn't dream of having anything that she doesn't already have. (eye roll)

The biggest problem is that I let her get to me.

Yeah, yeah... I know.... I have heard it before. So many will say that I need to forgive and forget. Well, FUCK that! I don't have to DO anything! My mom and dad don't really deserve it, in my opinion.

Why is this the first mention of my dad?

My dad was the enabler to my mother. He

would disappear a lot. Hunting, fishing, golf, charity work, or ANY excuse to be out of the house of horrors. He played outside with us sometimes. He taught us how to plant things, do yard work, which I still love to this day, and occasionally we would get to join him on one of his adventures. He made us feel like there was joy in the world. The problem with all of this was that he never stopped my mom.

Oh, he knew. I know this with 100% confidence. How? Well, I told him.

He was leaving the house one day in the summer on one of those particular days when the house was in chaos because of my mom's mood. I asked him not to leave because when he does, mom hits us and hurts us.

His answer? "Better you than me!" (exact words)

I was devastated. It was the actual moment that I knew there would never be a safe moment in my childhood home. I would have to remove myself from it completely. I would have to make my own life. I would have to make my own happiness. I would have to leave them behind to be happy. I would have to remain in survival mode until I could move past it all.

Moving on does not give them an out or complete forgiveness. It does mean that I won't have to rethink every motive behind a moment of kindness. I won't have to prepare my heart for betrayal and abuse. It means that when my past is behind me and I no longer let it stress my mind, I will be able to talk to and interact with these people as if they were strangers, if I even have to interact with them at all.

I still have siblings that live near them. I hope that one day I can visit for a holiday and really enjoy it. I CAN be kind without letting them into my life.... just how I would treat a stranger.

I don't seek out strangers and I won't seek out my parents either. It does make me sad. But, I must protect my own heart and soul. I must protect my mental health. It is my responsibility to myself and my family that I know truly love me.

CHAPTER 2

Chakra 2

****

I have been told that I can be overly sensitive, if there is such a thing. It is time for me to just be able to have the feelings I feel without reprimand or fear of hurt, pain, or shame. Because I rarely trust what people say, everything that is said to me is taken in, analyzed, and broken down for hidden meanings. That is the game I have played since I could understand. I don't know how to trust what is said. Too many times it has proven dangerous. That is the pattern I need to break now that I know that I am safe.

Unfortunately for my family, they don't know this game that I play with myself. Mostly, I do it with my husband. Poor guy. My three adult children are from my loins, so I KNOW them. As their mother, I am blessed to have spent their school years mostly at home. I was lucky enough to experience those years first hand.

I did work a few jobs. Mostly it was retail and only when we were settled enough for me to even try. During our marriage we moved a lot because of our military life, then because of federal law enforcement. Sometimes the job's pay didn't justify daycare. So, I stayed home.

I worked very hard to NOT be like my mother. I even told my husband before we got married that if he ever caught me acting like her, please let me know, and I will stop. So far, he may have called me out three times. Each time came early in our marriage. Luckily for me, I learn fast. I had to to survive as a child, a handy ability that I am proud to have.

At almost 50 years old now, I still struggle with the damage done by my mom. She is still alive, as is my dad. My therapist has offered to press charges against her because Maryland has no statute of limitations on the time to charge someone with child abuse. But, what good would that do?

When I think about them, I have to quickly remind myself that I am an adult and have the choice to interact with them. This is why I love that I live more than five states away. No surprise visits (as if that would even be a thing), and no one knows them in my town! Why is this important to me? A narcissist, like my mom, can and will use neighbors and friends to control their victim's environment. There is great freedom in that I don't have to worry about her manipulation in the community where I live.

I get sad sometimes when I think about what I have to do to be happy. What a conundrum!

Luckily for me, I go to therapy and have done enough research and soul searching to now know that this is and will always be my past. It is my life, all of the good and all of the bad. It is the bedrock of my life. And, just like every grand building or monument, the bedrock is unseen. It is a plain and unseen foundation to a life that will eventually become an amazing and a beautiful addition to this world and many lives.

That is where I want to end up.... a treasure and worthwhile memory... a beautiful reminder of a beautiful and wonderful life.

Isn't that what we all hope for?

But first, I have to deal with my body's manifestation of this past. I have to clean and clear out the crud that is keeping me from the vision that I want to become a reality.

****

I suffer from depression.

Surprised? Me, neither. Alyssa, the gold standard therapist, informed me that I also suffer from Chronic Childhood Post Traumatic Stress Disorder (CPTSD). I guess I should have known that was a thing. But growing up in the 70's and 80's, the only time you heard of PTSD was when talking about war veterans. They called it Shell Shock for a long time until they figured out that the damage to the brain is different with different traumas and often presents itself in different ways and intensities.

I detest depression. IT SUCKS! The void...the nothingness...the lack of feeling and care for myself....or anything else that should make me happy or at least content. There is nothing. And for some reason, everything seems to hurt but it also doesn't matter at the same time. I don't even recall my dreams when I am deep in the void.

I have been on numerous medications trying to balance out my brain chemistry. The latest one seems to be mild, yet effective. I am currently on the generic version of Cymbalta. I remain on this because medical assistance is needed until I am supernatural. I will make sure that my doctors are aware of my journey. I will not remove a medicine without my doctor's okay.

My other affliction, CPTSD, LOVES to get all up in my dreams and screw with me. It isn't treated with medication. This is something that I must work through. Once I do, maybe those horrible dreams that I do remember will cease, or at least change for the better.

Those damn dreams!

I have had the same theme of being deserted or abandoned by my husband for many months. He is the ONLY consistent source of love I have had. Plus, he chose and still chooses to love me. When I have one of these dreams, it can hurt sometimes to the bone. Those dreams haunt me for hours and sometimes, days!

I am fortunate that my husband acts like he actually cares about my feelings.

Here is what I just said…. He ACTS like he actually cares.

I want to believe that he does, I truly and confidently want to believe. But, that leaves me open to be really hurt. And HE could REALLY hurt me. He has my heart, with its scars, bruises, and withered spots that are scabbed over and healing. He somehow finds it beautiful. I honestly don't know what he is seeing but I am glad he sees it. Maybe he is my karma? Do I deserve such a love? I hope someday, I feel like I do. I want to be everything for him, AND everything to myself.

But, How?

How am I being fair to him? Doesn't he deserve a whole person? Doesn't he deserve a love that makes him feel the way he makes me feel? Absolutely.

I am a greedy human though. I would never give him up. He is my secret gold nugget. My found treasure. I want to horde him. I don't

want to share my nugget. Unfortunately, I
don't get a say in that. He has a much greater
purpose on this earth than to be my favorite
treasure. He is such a good human. I don't
mean a good man. I mean a GOOD HUMAN!
Any man or woman would be exemplary if they
had his mind and capacity for good.

He IS a good man, too. Actually, he is GREAT!
The things that come to mind when I think of a
man are presented in him in the most beautiful
arrangement of cells and DNA. My goodness,
but he is beautiful. So incredibly yummy! And
if I told you that my pleasure is his TOP
priority, there would be no lightening strikes to
worry about. MMMMmmm. He's yummy.

Yes, he distracts me with his yumminess. I am
a lover of beautiful things. And he is the most
beautiful of all, inside and out.

He thinks that I exaggerate when I say this, but
he has his own human issues to deal with too. I
just hope that he believes me and feels it when
I tell him of the depth of the love I have for
him. I may sound like I am bragging, but I am
just aware of him... all of him.

When I think of the life that I have gotten to share with him, I feel joy. He helped me create three beautifully imperfect children that we have brought into this world together. We have two amazing sons and an amazing daughter born between them. They are the most wonderful gifts to me and anyone they meet. I found that I got to be the mom that they needed, not the one that I needed. I am not my mom and even if she had been a perfect mom, I still wouldn't be like her.

When I became a mom, the world opened for me. I got to watch these beautiful humans grow, smile, laugh, and love. I got to be there when they had boo-boos or had a mean kid mess with them. Every one of them had a problem with bullies. They handled them all in different ways. They each got to learn from their siblings how to handle an argument. My kids rarely argued but they did learn from, not just their own interactions with people, but from their siblings' interactions as well.

I loved watching them discover and learn. I loved being a sounding board for them through the years. They still come to me for advice. This is something that I take pride in. I never had this kind of closeness with my parents. It is nice. Even if I am seeing it from the mom side of things for now.

I think my husband gets a little upset that they don't go to him first. I think it is because he likes to fix things and I am just listening and bouncing off ideas. I basically leave the decision up to them on what they should do. It isn't just because I want them to know what to do, but because they need to think it through. Consequences for their actions are theirs alone to deal with.

What I mean by that is that whether the results are good or bad, it is on them. They can't blame anyone but themselves. I find that that is the easiest way for me in life as well. Some situations may result in big rewards or big disappointment. If a person can have an out and can blame someone else for hardships, then what have they learned?

If I succeeded in something, would I want my hard work to be claimed by another? Hell No! That is the same as blaming someone else for a bad decision and resulting hardship. It isn't their karma to work through.

This may be yet another way I protect myself. It makes my decisions all mine. I know there is no question of trust, blame, or validity. There is no question of motive nor intent by anyone else. It is in my control.

Maybe this is why my dreams, or should I say nightmares, get to me. I have no control over anything. I can't stop my husband from leaving and I don't know why he does it. I don't know where my deficiency lies. What action in my life resulted in him leaving?

It haunts me.

Let me share what I mean.

*************** "The Dream…"
****

The theme is always the same, but the location and time line changes. Our age also changes in the dream, sometimes during the dream.

It starts off that we are home. The kids are of school age and we are in some kind of transition in our lives. The first dream had us exiting the military and living in a new home.

Not the home we are in now, but a conglomerate of our previous houses.

We are just settling in after going to the store or something. I am sitting on the bed. I am talking to him. He walks in the room. He is in his military uniform, stops in the doorway, and looks at me. His face falls showing NO emotion, then he says, "I'm done!" He turns around, walks down the stairs, grabs his keys and his drivers license and walks out the front door, cranks his new truck that we just got, and drives away. He doesn't take his wallet, his cell phone or any other possession.

He leaves me and the kids. I end up searching for two years before I find him. I had huge struggles after he left.I had no car because he took our only vehicle, the house we had just moved into had to be given back to the bank.

My husband left me with the only access to our bank as well as his future retirement or disability monthly check. So, that means he didn't leave because he wanted all of the money. It means that he didn't want me or anything that I brought into his life. It is a crushing feeling and it can still haunt me. The majority of my dreams start here with me looking for him and feeling the shattering blow of him not loving me.

I beg for the kids, I beg for me. I would do anything to get him back. He is my love.

When the dreams have him with someone else, it is even worse. I KNOW that when my husband loves, he loves with his whole heart. This is just another way for me to see that he will never love me again.....because he has found love again.

It is horrible. I hate it. I truly HATE it.

When am I going to stop having this damn dream? What emotion do I need to be aware of to sleep and dream the good stuff?

I want to get back to dreaming of what I'd do if I won the lottery. This is my go to dream, like counting sheep.

(*Unless, the universe thinks that it is time to let me win the actual lottery, then, by all means, Universe, rain down the fun. In this day and age, that is how the common man gets "rich,"or for most in this country, this is the actual "American dream." Unless we want to become part of the system… just another cog in the machine…. The Lottery would give us the freedom to give to and enjoy the world without need of another… Isn't that funny? It take MILLIONS of people spending money for one to win. That is just the way it is. I hope I get a turn…)(fingers crossed)

CHAPTER 3

Chakra 3

****
*

I want everything and nothing.

I want everything that is good and nothing
that is bad. Is this possible? How do we make
the world all good in our own mind? Are there
even people who think like this? I don't yet,
but would like to.

There doesn't seem to be just one path. I
don't know if aligning my chakras, meditation,
yoga, ayahuasca, THC, or anything else can
clear my mind of the damage and roadblocks in
my emotional growth. I am willing to try, and
have tried, just about anything.

I am just now learning the in's and out's of the
Chakra aligning. With its many meanings and
uses, it intrigues me that maybe there is a bit
of magic in us.

Ah, to be magic. This is something we have
witnessed in movies, but never in real life. I

would imagine, if asked, most humans would want to be able to manipulate energy, make potions that actually work, and all of the fantastical different nuances of magic that we see in our fantasies, myths, and ancient tales that are the basis for many of the movies we love.

I truly believe that we were meant to be able to have our own forms of magic. Each person using their ability, talent, skills, and knowledge in conjunction with another to make this world all that it was meant to be.

Is it so hard to believe?

All my life, I have felt that I am constrained… like my energy has a straight jacket on. I can feel that I should be able to have free flowing energy to share, heal, love, explore, energize and stimulate.

There is something I am meant to do, but I am struggling to reveal it. I feel a pull or urge to keep searching.

Maybe our "God gene" is misunderstood? Maybe the message of Jesus's life was to show us that God (or a greater power) lives in us all. Maybe Jesus wanted us to harness our potential and advance our species. Maybe he was just a man who reached his true human potential.

It makes sense to me more and more when I start reading, watching, researching and discovering the tales that were hidden from all of us. The written folklore that we all know must hold elements of truth to them. This has to be evident in the many repeat elements in those tales. I feel like I need to question everything about the information from our past on this Earth.

But, I digress….

It took me a while to figure out where to go from here. I had been without a therapist for almost two years since Alyssa's retirement. I started backsliding in my emotional growth. I thought I was as far as I was going to get with dealing with my trauma and thought that maybe I could go it alone, But I couldn't. I had almost returned to my pre-Alyssa state. So I conceded and started asking about therapists with my psychiatrist. After a trial with another therapist that didn't feel right, I found Katie! How did I get so lucky to have won the Therapist lottery, twice? Katie has taken me from backsliding in my journey to strapping emotional rockets to my soul. She has helped me take leaps and bounds in a very short time.

Once I felt more like I was back on the right track, I stumbled upon a Gaia show by Dr. Joe Dispenza. His name sounded familiar. I searched my books and found that I own the book that is the basis for the show. It is in my "to read," stack. Coincidence? Well, maybe not. If I am to believe that we manifest our own worlds and have elements inside of us that would be seen as magic to the common eye, I can't believe that coincidence is even a real thing.

I learned in just the first episode that I am not who I am meant to be.

First, I live in the past. EVERY DAY!

This has to stop for me to reach the unknown ME of the future. The ME that I know that I can and want to be.

My every thought stems from my past. Every feeling, emotion, reaction, and instinct was ingrained in me from birth and conditioned in trauma. I need to rewire my brain to think the way I want. To build new memories for my brain to draw from that will build the foundation of the new ME.

What a strange circle. I must use my brain to rewire....my brain.

Maybe then I will be able to have those magical powers that I want so badly.

Isn't there a saying that goes, "If you can imagine it, you can create it?"

Well, I guess it is time for me to get cracking. I am more than willing to erase connections to my past to reach the now and learn for my future.

It is my understanding that this doesn't just apply to the mind. It is supposed to work for the body as well. So, maybe I can learn to better my body through my mind.

For a person with autoimmune disorders and mental chemical imbalance, any and all improvement is most welcome in my life.

Here's to hoping!

CHAPTER 4

****

**

Let's get started!

Time to become the ME that I have always known was waiting to emerge.

It seems easy and difficult at the same time but I am ready.

I need to rewire my mind and brain. Those things sound the same but they aren't. The mind is our ability to think outside of the situation. Our inner monologue, so to speak. It is the part of thinking that is separate from the situation at hand. Our brain knows what to do without being told.

Breathe! (my brain: I am)

Walk! (I am)

Scratch that itch! (I get it!)

I didn't have to think before I did them. My body just knew what to do. Of course, I am in control the whole time It is just that my mind doesn't have to expel extra energy or give extra attention to those type of things. It is second nature.

That is the goal for rewiring my brain. Making those happy thoughts, body movement, and energy direction something that my body sees as natural. These things should be in the same category as breathing or walking. This is something that I want my brain to see as ME. I don't want to have to struggle and think through stress to have these things. I want my body to be able to redirect my stress levels to return to normal after each stress trigger. The good doctor Dispenza says that THAT is the first step. Learn to recognize and consciously redirect our focus to stop the stress hormone and its results on the body.

Wow. Sounds simple, right?

I have to be smarter than my brain and body.

I need to learn to deep meditate, rethink, rewire, and direct my intentions which will eventually lead to the manifestations of my path, health, body, and personality changes.

In essence, I need to make my inner world my outer world!

How do I begin?

Dr. Dispenza gives an example of what your mind should feel like when you put your brain into "alpha wave" style thinking.

If you have ever driven a car and reached your destination without actually remembering the whole drive because you were off in your own mind and your body took over the task of driving and obeying road laws while you were drifting in your thoughts, then you have achieved your alpha wave level of thinking. This is the first step in reaching that level where "You are conscious in your subconscious."

Huh, who knew? I have done this so many times.

Now to learn how to do it intentionally, so that I can start to ascend.

I have envisioned my future self in "bliss."

The vision is so beautiful and in the vision, my life is just happy and fulfilling. I see myself. Theo, my husband, is there. Why wouldn't he be? He is my love. He is in the vision but doesn't influence it. This is about me.

Wow. This.... is.... about.... me.

This is my world.

He can envision his own bliss.

Now. How do I remove my feelings of selfishness that has been conditioned into me by my trauma?

First, It is NOT selfish. It is NOT narcissistic to want better for myself. Second, it is that trauma/scar that makes me think this way. I need to see myself without that scar, because the time for possible re-injury is over.

When I think about it, wouldn't this betterment trickle through my whole life like an echo or a ripple? If I raise my vibration or level of consciousness, those around me will either get on board or be left at the station.

CHAPTER 5

Chakra 4

****

***

Is it harsh to cut people out of my life? (Or leave them at the station?) It feels that way right now. It feels like I am killing them.

In a way, I am. They will not be the same to me. They will be removed from influence in my mind and placed in the "stranger" category. Do I remember every stranger I have met? No. BUT, I do remember the feelings of the interactions. They will be listed under lessons learned. Is there a mention of forgiveness or acceptance? NO. A stranger is not given access to that level of personal feelings.

The parents that I grew up with are in my past. They will never have the power to manipulate me again unless I let them.

No, I do not go "home" for the holidays. No, I do not call them unless it is to say happy birthday or for a holiday like Christmas. I left that home at 19 years old. Until recently, I didn't realize it but, that is when I started becoming me.

I have stepped out of that life. I unzipped that suit and stepped out of it. I became a raw newborn at that moment, emotionally and spiritually. I discovered that I had my own power.

I became a free human when I joined the military. It was scary and uncharted waters for me. My life and existence was entirely in my control for the first time. As that newborn, I made mistakes. But, those mistakes taught me about consequence and how my actions can affect the direction of my life and sometimes those closest to me.

The only person that came with me on this journey was Theo. He was there when my consequences came back to bite me in the butt. It almost left me alone. He almost left me. I have never been more thankful for his big loving heart than I was at that moment.

My era of trial and error left a stain on the new life that I longed for. Unfortunately, it also hurt the only person who has ever loved the real me.

He still loves the real me. He has watched me struggle and accept my responsibility for my actions. He has stuck with me through it all. I am VERY aware of it and could NOT be more grateful for him.

He has never tried to rule over me. He has never tried to hurt me either. Well, not in any way that I didn't deserve.(never physical pain) He was well in his rights to make me earn his trust. It is the greatest regret of my life....hurting him.

In this journey, I am supposed to be able to let go of stresses to grow.

I honestly believe that if a person takes responsibility for their actions and genuinely apologizes to those who were hurt, they can become more and grow. That doesn't mean that the other person needs to accept that apology. It means that I can move on. It is not my responsibility to help them grow past the hurt. Even though I caused it, I can't erase the wounds. I may be able to lessen the scar but it will always be there.

That is the part that I have to live with. It has been acknowledged, dealt with, and forgiven. It is the "forgiven" part that I have such a problem with.

I don't know how to accept forgiveness. It feels like a new concept.

As a child, I was taught to apologize for my wrongs. It was brought to my attention. It was sometimes forced on me after a fight with a sibling or even after receiving a beating. Apologizing in front of or to a narcissist mother gave her power over me. It was always a fight for control with me. I was a very smart but headstrong child. I didn't like to take the blame for something that wasn't my fault. I also didn't want to take the entire blame when it should be shared.

This led to many struggles of will in my house. I would take the beating, as if I had a choice, if it meant not apologizing for something I didn't do. This led to a lot of trauma in many forms. That strong will was going to put me in a hospital or grave. I needed to be smarter.

I didn't want my mom to think that I was conceding to guilt or admitting to doing something that I didn't do. So the beating would continue until I broke.

I learned to fake cry. I had to. I practiced to be convincing. I managed to go from maybe 10 licks or more with whatever instrument she managed to choose to deliver her wrath to about three. It seemed like a good number to make it believable. I could handle three. I would walk away with a smile in my mind knowing she didn't get what she wanted out of me.

There was NEVER a time when my parents taught forgiveness. How could they? They didn't know how to teach something they had no intention of ever using.

This is why I struggle. I had to figure out what that meant. Forgiveness.

CHAPTER 6

Chakra 5

****
**

Forgiveness is such a loaded yet simple word.

After having children it seemed easy.

I looked at their little faces and KNEW that
they would always have a safe place with me. I
would not ruin them. Or at least I would be the
kind of parent that I wanted growing up. I
wanted to be what they needed.

Of course, as a parent, it is all trial and error
until you figure out basic parenting skills.

Yes, I see them as basic.

It should be expected in every child's life that
they have food, shelter, love, and safety. This
means that only worldly possessions are
excluded. It is not necessary to have
everything to be a happy child. This has been

seen time and time again.

It was so clear to me what I needed to provide. Why isn't it clear to everyone, especially those that become parents? Why do we have child abuse in our world? It is sickening to think of the children in history that had to survive their childhoods and the atrocities done to them by the people that they should be able to trust the most and feel safe around.

I am not a perfect parent but I am a dang good one. I will never take that from myself.I was lucky to have the type of mind that usually thinks things through before starting them. Parenting was no different.

By doing this, I got to watch what a childhood was supposed to look like. I witnessed it through my children. I watched what happens to a person when they grow up in a safe environment. By "safe," I mean loved so deeply that they get to be free to be who they were always meant to be. I just guided them and accepted them.

I always told them that I would never hold their teenage and hormone driven words against them. NEVER! I wanted them to know that they were allowed to make mistakes in this world but could always come home. They could be angry, or confused. They could be ridiculous. They knew that I would always love them. Those teenage years are the most important, in my opinion.

They were told that whatever decision that they made was theirs; theirs to reap the benefits or pay the consequences. Their choices could hurt others too so they had to keep that in mind.

I also taught them to apologize. But this needs to be secondary to the importance of forgiveness. Without forgiveness, negativity can fester until it affects other areas of your body or life.

Sounds like an easy lesson, right?

Well, it is easy to say or write. It is a lot easier to teach it to your child than it is to deal with as an adult.

This is a lesson that I am learning now.

****

**

My body, mind, and spirit have taken the hit from my life.

I am overweight, depressed, have less than good health, suffer from autoimmune diseases and have had numerous injuries and surgeries.

Until recently, I thought that this was how it was going to be until I left this world.

Not anymore. It is time to become the me that I was always meant to be.

This new me may be nothing like the old me. For one, the old me was in survival mode. It was carrying all of that confusion and hurt. After seemingly stumbling upon the book by Dr Dispenza, and then actually finding it in television form, I knew it was a message meant for me.

The new me wants to be free. Free to be me without judgement.

I want to bloom for the rest of my life.

I want to be a beautiful example of a human

life.

I have to stop worrying about what others will think of the new me. Will they find me ridiculous? Will they think I am crazy? Will they continue to want to be a part of my life? How will they accept me? What if society thinks I am a misfit? What if I am too much for others?

I have to condition myself to say, "I don't care what you or anyone else thinks!"

This is MY life. This is MY path through the cosmos. This is MY path to make. I am nothing and everything in it.

Why shouldn't this chunk of star stuff feel accepted in this world?

Society says that we have to act a certain way, be a certain way, live a certain way. But society doesn't live in my brain. It doesn't know my unique life path. Hell, society doesn't know, nor should it have a say in my "becoming."

Now it is time to figure out who I want to be. What do I want to accomplish in this life?

Oh, and is there a way to actually become supernatural? What does that even mean?

Is it like that famous wizard series written by a very creative British woman? Or is it just our own ability to move past our own past to manifest and make happen our future?

One sounds awesome and the other sounds like a lot of work…but, MAN, I want them! Both of them!

Who am I? Or who is this hidden person that is ready to face the world? What words do I want to describe me? What is my personality?

Let's start with the basics and see where it leads.

What is a personality? The dictionary says that it is the combination of characteristics or qualities that form an individual's distinctive character. (Google)

In other definitions it includes: sets of behaviors, cognitions, and emotional patterns that evolve from biological and environmental factors.

So by cutting out my past personality and all of its factors, I can start with a clean slate. No need for survival mode. No need for feeling unloved and unsafe.

Wow! That sounds great! I have never felt completely safe before. My tainted past has always kept its wool over my eyes.

Now I am free to be. Free to be happy. Free to love, my way.

That is a big realization for me. Why have I let others dictate how I feel? Is it that people pleasing resulted from the trauma of being raised the way I was? Absolutely.

I want to say that I need to put myself first, but I don't like the way that makes me feel. This is a result of my abusive childhood. Being raised by an abusive narcissist conditioned me to be that people pleaser and still feel like any action that went against those conditions, was, in essence, selfish.

****
**

CHAPTER 7

Many people who claim childhood trauma sometimes worry that they will never be believed by anyone if they expose their abuser. I worry about that as well.

I shouldn't because this gives my abuser power over me. That power is in the form of FEAR.

I have also heard that the mind makes up things that aren't true.

PHYSICAL ABUSE IS NOT ONE OF THEM. Abuse that involves the mind is more complicated and even though not as evident, is more damaging.

The abuser will say, "I didn't do/say that." or "You are crazy.""You are making things up." "That never happened." "You are exaggerating. It wasn't that bad."

Well, It is not up for debate anymore.

Lucky for me I have proof from outside of my family. I say "lucky" because I don't have to worry about being confused or invalidated. I will never have to ask myself, "Am I remembering things correctly?" I have friends that can back me up.

I found out just a couple of years ago that my abuser did a horrible thing to a close life long friend's wonderful mother.

Despite my home environment, school was a place that I loved. Maybe not because of the classes and things that I learned but because I felt safe to be me. Well, more me than I got to be at home. I held so much of myself back. I presented a strong exterior to the masses.

There were only a couple of friends that knew what was happening. One of those friends, who is still a friend to this day, told her mother. Her mother was an amazing woman. She was so sweet, so loving and just a beautiful soul.

My friend and her family were in the same socioeconomic category as we were. They survived but were not the type to have extra anything.

This beautiful and humble woman, Ms. Audrey, helped me load up my stuff and move it to her house during a day when my mom was at work and I was the only one home. I was 19 at the time and decided that it was time for me to escape. I was going to be moving in with my friend...her daughter.

She was a newlywed and had a mobile home that had an extra bedroom. She rented it out to me and let me borrow her extra car to get back and forth to work. Her husband was going to be away for months at Army basic training. I had signed up for the Air Force and would be going to my own basic training in less than 6 months. I was also dating the guy who would become my husband.

It was the first time that anyone helped me. I didn't think that there was a soul out there that would actually listen and believe me.

My mom had a good status at our church and the majority of people I interacted with went to that church. In a small southern town, being a member and going to a church is sometimes the only social setting with gatherings and interactions that happen outside of school. Ms

Audrey went to my church. Yet, she believed me. I guess my mom's mask had slipped off one too many times in front of her. What ever it was that opened her eyes, was a blessing.

I did end up going into the Air Force. I trained in Biloxi, Mississippi, in a now obsolete form of Satellite Communications. This gave me time with my boyfriend who was still in school in our Mississippi hometown.

I turned 20 the year that I was training in Biloxi. When I got my first duty station to go to New Mexico, I had to collect all of my stuff that was still at my childhood home and at my friend's house because I would only be back for visits. While between assignments and gathering my things, the beautiful Ms Audrey died in a car accident. Her life was tragically cut short. Her beautiful family was shattered. I wanted to stay. I wanted to grieve. But, I had to leave. Her family would have to lay her to rest without my support. I still wish I could have been there.

Fast forward to a couple of years ago. I live near the nation's capital. My friend had a chance to come up to my area with her husband for his work. We met up at her hotel and took the metro to the zoo for the day. I brought my daughter who had recently graduated high school. It was a fun day trip.

While we were catching up, my friend got real serious and nervous. She said that she had to tell me that she was "sorry."

I was confused.

"Why are you sorry?"

"I was so mean to you when you lived with me."

"No, you weren't."

"Yes, I was. My mom called me shortly after you moved in and told me that your mom confronted her and told her that it was all her (Ms Audrey's) fault that you moved out and that her family is broken. Mom told me to try to get you to go home on your own by making it difficult."

I looked at her in shock, anger, shame, sadness, and disbelief. I have NEVER been more angry at my mother. How DARE SHE!!!

That would mean that THAT BEAUTIFUL WOMAN went to her death with that on her shoulders and mind.

My mom KNEW who was at blame for my moving out because I left her a letter telling her and my dad EXACTLY why I was leaving. She had NO excuse to blame Ms Audrey. I wanted to vomit. I wanted to cry. This had been on my friend's mind since 1993. Twenty-eight years of grief and regret. Twenty-eight!!

I looked at my friend. She sat in front of me with embarrassment and shame on her face. I wanted to hug her. I looked her in the face and told her that she had never made me feel unwelcome. Adding a bit of humor, I told her, "If that was you being mean, you suck at it!" Her mouth fell open.

I started laughing which lightened the air. "I grew up with a narcissist mom who KNEW how to be mean. I didn't even realize you were doing it." She looked at me and asked, "Really?"

"Really. Don't fret over this for one more second. You did nothing wrong. I want to also apologize for my mother. I am so sorry that you have been dealing with this all of these years."

She is such a wonderful friend. Maybe even one of the souls that I have known before. I am lucky to have had such wonderful friends from my childhood. They are all beautiful and intelligent beings who enrich my life. They are the good that came from a bad time.

I cried for Ms Audrey. I wanted so badly to apologize to her. Not for talking to her, telling her my secrets, nor accepting her help. No. her actions were pure.

I wanted to apologize for my mother. I wish I would have known before her death. I would have lifted that off of her mind. She did not deserve that. She will always be my hero in the truest sense of the word. She helped me escape! She is one of a few wonderful women that I have used as an example of how to be a truly loving mother.

I would like to praise and acknowledge these women for their part in my life. Their names are Audrey, Peggy (Aunt), Audrey (not the

same), and Isley Elizabeth (my Maw-Maw).
They each deserve to have their names out
there for the world to know.

****
**

There was a span of about two weeks, right
before I left for basic, that I went home. I
wanted to say goodbye to my younger
siblings. They didn't deserve the wrath that
surely came down on them after I left. This
was wrath that I was all too familiar with after
my older sister became a teenage mom who
had a shotgun wedding.

I love my siblings. Without them, I would not
have made it through that childhood. I was
damaged but not completely broken.

Of course, I knew my abuser would try to
deceive me while I was there. The pattern is
always there. She would be nice, warm up to
me, talk softly, keep a pleasant face, and act
like she wants to know me, to be close to me.
Then I'd give a little of myself. I'd tell her a
little about my life or show her the smallest bit
of trust. This is her moment when she'd strike.

She'd twist my story or somehow make me feel stupid or shameful or just not as good as her.

She is the parent. I am supposed to submit to and support her views, attitude and most of all, her authority. This is her pattern, to this day. This is why she will forever be a stranger if I MUST interact with her. I will not allow her into my life again.

I look back on that time and think about how easy it was for my mother to do that to someone else and act like it never happened. I guess she thought she won. Ms Audrey never had the chance to tell me. I know that she would have eventually because I would have made a point to visit her over the years. My mom never mentioned it, naturally. Why would a narcissist think that she was wrong?

Even as I am writing this I am dealing with her latest jab at "putting me in my place." My mother recently had cosmetic surgery. She had her hanging stomach skin removed. I too suffer from hanging stomach from a bad first pregnancy with later resulting obesity and skin that lacked the proper elasticity. What does she do? If you know how an abusive narcissists works, you know that she had to make sure that I knew how happy she was. After a few weeks of recovery, and no call from me to check on her. She wanted me to be jealous. I was at first. I have to admit. Then I realized where my mind was going. So I thought of her as a stranger sharing something that makes them happy. It really cleared my head. I actually hope that the surgery helps her.

She has always done this sort of thing to me. When Theo and I were in the military and he was sent to the other side of the world, I was left alone to raise our children. If I expressed my sadness or stress about the separation or the fear that my husband could die, I would get, "Well, you chose the life. Deal with it!"

A few years later, while we were still in the military, my mom chose to take part in a promotional opportunity for her job that required her to commute out of state for the week and come home on the weekends for over a span of a year. During this time, she called my phone crying about how much she missed my dad during the week. She wanted me to console her. I know! The audacity!

Narcissism isn't all I had to deal with. As if that wasn't enough, she was an abuser in many forms. She abused me physically as well. Many times I had bruises and large welts. This came pretty regularly yet random. I am not talking about spanking or swatting. Although, I don't condone that anymore, spanking or swatting a child should have been done under the spirit of a safety or correction lesson. She would almost explode with rage. There were times that I was awakened with a beating or tossed around by the hair. She is lucky that she never broke my neck with the aggressive shaking of my head by means of a hand full of my hair. Her abuse was filled with a level of malevolence that would frighten any child, and apparently husbands.

I had gone to school with clear signs. If anyone asked what happened, I would tell them in hopes that they would report her. I felt safer at school than at home. It always came as a shock to whomever I told. Nothing was ever done. I went to school in the late 70's and graduated in 1990.

Abuse and abusers weren't talked about. People didn't have to give the school permission to paddle your child. Parents got away with so many things.

I always hoped that someone would come save me and let me move out of her house. Summers were a bitch when we had to be inside the house when our mom was home on one of her more evil days.

After some of the beating episodes she would warn us that we would get it even worse when she returned home, if we ever called the cops on her. I have come to find that that is a common phrase used by abusers.

All of this made me want to leave...just escape. When I did, I felt like a lost wanderer who didn't know anything about myself. I know now that I didn't know myself because I was a free soul for the first time. I got to make my own choices without her influence. It was a strange, scary, and amazing feeling.

But, it has taken me until now to feel like I am on the right path in this journey called life.

I can't say I don't still have a little fear when I think of my mother. I am still a work in progress. But, I have come to realize that there is nothing she can do to me. NOTHING. I am a full grown person and have a beautiful family that loves me and supports me. They are all that matter to me in this world.

If my mom read this, would it hurt her feelings?

That is not my problem. If the truth finally coming out hurts, then it is a pain she needs to figure out on her own. I am still dealing with the scars she left on my being. My soul's memory is far longer and runs deeper than any of the bruises left.

I know that over the years that I have been away from my hometown and my extended family, my mother has filled any ear that would entertain her about me. I know this. Such is the way of an abusive narcissist. I have been told by the wonderful few who see through her and don't believe her.

Maybe because they have spent five minutes getting to know me.

So, I know that if anyone who knows her reads

this, apart from her children and spouse, they may not believe me. That is okay. This is not written for any kind of approval nor belief in my life story. I am not trying to win anyone to "my side." This is not up for debate nor is it part of a smear tactic. This is my journey to know myself and to become more.

And, there is MORE to me than my trauma. So much more.

I have studied, researched, read, practiced and done a number of things to get to this point.

I have been searching for myself everywhere. I have been researching my family tree for over 20 years, taken every quiz that crossed my path, read numerous self help books and psychology based books. I have studied my astrology charts, energy flows, blood type, genetic links, DNA break down, personality types and many other avenues that would mold me in some different way.

Wether it is with diet, exercise, education, recognition and acceptance of my emotions or

any other way to make myself better, I
welcomed it. I have also seen a therapist for a
few years and a psychiatrist for depression.

CHAPTER 8

****
*

What do I want?

I want to be happy and free. I want my body to do what I want and move the way I want. I want my emotions to be under complete control but not stifled.

I want to love myself. I want to love my body. I want to look at myself and see what I know intellectually is amazing but have yet to engrain into my being. I want to know my worth.

I want to be free to express myself without the fear of upsetting someone else because it isn't about them.

I want to voice my needs without feeling like I am being selfish.

I want to move, to explore, and to have adventures of all kinds.

I want to laugh. I want to find joy and humor in life.

I want to be simple but supernatural at the same time.

I want to design and build my life to reflect the inner me. I want to be creative.

I want to know life's secrets. I want to know the unknowable. I want to be able to manipulate energy. I want to fly. I would love to be able to pause time and travel to other dimensions too.

I want to be a spiritual witch type person for lack of a better term. I want to be able to commune with spirits, see auras, and have the ability of divination. I want to be able to control the elements. I want real powers.

I also want to be beautiful. I don't think I am ugly by any means but I want to be striking! I want to stop people in their tracks with my beauty. Not necessarily outer beauty but a beauty that radiates from within. I want happiness clearly visible on my face.

I want to be a sexual creature…a completely

comfortable in my skin and with my desires kind of sexual creature.

I absolutely love sex.

I have always been sexual but I kept it hidden, like most, because of the "rules" of society. I want to live beyond that as I have stated. This includes sex and its many pleasures.

As a young child, I was aware of the pleasure of touch. Like all kids, I explored myself, but with shame. I didn't feel complete satisfaction until I was well into my marriage. As a people pleaser, I always thought that as long as my man finished, I did my part. And let's be honest, that is quite pleasurable too. BUT…not even close to knowing what my body is capable of.

I had many years of separation from my husband through deployments with the military and later with work. I was alone for many months; four years total. I had to figure it out on my own. Once I did, marriage got even better for both of us!

The utter satisfaction of amazing and orgasmic

sex is, well...perfection. A feeling that doesn't live in my head! Of course, the mind can influence it, but DAMN! It is amazing to have ONE organ that is for pleasure ONLY!! Men don't get to say this and I am not sure, but I think other females of other species are like our men. Well, I hope they get pleasure but that is not my field of expertise. I will leave that up to some scientist to figure out.

My sweet spouse has been able to show me that I can have freedom in being my true feminine self. I didn't know that that is all I have ever wanted.

To be free to be me.

I am a female. I love being a female!

I love having the ability to have babies, nurture, and mold complete human beings. I love the softness of being female. I love my breasts and entire bottom half. I love the power that comes with having a vagina. It is so amazing. There is something so beautifully raw and delicious about sex.

Just to be clear. I am not talking about love.

The term "making love" makes me want to gag. It sounds gross and false. Love, to me, is what is done outside the bedroom that leads to complete and utter surrender in the bedroom.

I love surrendering to my husband. I can give him complete trust during sex. He is pure masculine perfection.

My beautiful man has been trained in the military and also federal law enforcement in many lethal ways. He has been trained in ways that most guys can only dream of or only get a glimpse of in movies. He is physically strong. Watching him use that strength is like watching a superhero.

He is always fair and uses his intellect over emotions. He is highly educated yet openminded. He is hard when he needs to be but he can be surprisingly soft too. He is everything that I am not. He gives me everything I could ever want in a partner. I can be completely female with confidence.

I am glad and slightly upset that it took so long for me to discover this. If we, as a species, can get out of our own way, and work through our trust and fear issues, we would find that sex and experimenting with sex is natural and amazing... if you are ready and understanding enough to express it in a healthy and non-criminal way.

I have noticed in my discovery that many people still have to hide their level of human sexual openness. Society is still a "cock block," for lack of a better description. Many people are on a higher sexual or more open path than I am and more power to them! I hope they have a partner or partners that make them feel free and safe to be and give pleasure during sex.

My only hope is that I bring my husband the same if not more pleasure than he brings me. This may be " I MI," but I am done with blocking my healthy and positive thoughts. This is just part of the new me.

I am so glad that I met Theo when I did. His moral compass kept me from diving feet first into debauchery. I honestly think that if his love had not entered my life when it did, I would have thrown my body to the winds!

I married a wise old soul who I know was meant for me. I believe in that sort of thing. I believe completely. I truly believe he has been my soul mate for many lifetimes and in many forms. I think that he followed me into this life. He was born three years after me and had he been born any other time, I don't know if it would have worked so wonderfully.

We were teens. I was 19 and he was 16. Had he been older than me, I probably would not have trusted him. Had he been in the same class in school with me, I would have overlooked him because I was in survival mode in high school.

It was a slight scandal (maybe in my own mind) that I was dating someone younger. I knew this. It took me a whole week to say yes to his request to go on a date. His existence had hit me like a bullet straight to my heart, mind, soul, and body! I had thought other guys were intriguing or attractive in some way, but never like this. Never had I seen this perfect combination of traits in such an attractive package.

He is still just as gorgeous. Naturally tan, fit,

with gorgeous green eyes, masculine yet gentle, loving, not afraid to be silly, intelligent, confident, hard working, always wants to see me naked, wants to bring me pleasure and happiness and wants to be with me as much as possible. Who could ask for anything better?

He was so young, yet so perfect for me. If there is a God, let me say this for the record. THANK YOU for creating this beautiful human and introducing him to me when you knew I would notice! He is perfectly imperfect and sexy as all get out! He has my whole soul in his hands and I am his forever.

My sexual life has grown with my maturity. It has evolved properly. It is actually one of the only areas in my life that I feel was not affected by my childhood trauma.

I seem on par with most other people at this stage in their lives. Even though I am now considered to be going into my "crone" stage.

Let me just say, I don't care for that word because of the image that pops in my head. (You know, the witch from Saturday morning cartoons growing up... She was green, round around the middle, and every time she flew away on her broomstick, she always left bobby-pins in the air.)

I want to make this word into something else. I want to embrace my age and desires and bring a new meaning to this unattractive sounding word.

I want to live in my feminine...all the way in it, all the time. I want to bring beauty to this world.

Granted, I have created three wonderful and beautiful beings that I hope change this world for the better. Those were my biggest creations. Anything made by hand pales in comparison. So, what do I have to be afraid of? Nothing!!

I have many talents. I can sing, dance, play an instrument, read music. Anything musical draws me. It has such power in its vibrations. I've also done a little acting too.

I can draw, paint, solder, build things, and have a mind for solving problems. I can cook and sew. I can create and do many forms of arts and crafts.

I am an excellent organizer and can clean like a fiend when I have the energy. (Thanks, Air Force!) I have great spacial awareness and can design and decorate, which is one of my career/school pursuits.

I am an amazing photographer. I have shot many topics but my favorite thing to capture is the beauty of life and nature. I have had a couple of my travel shots published in a local magazine. It isn't huge but it makes me proud.

I like to make up songs for my babies and fur babies. I think I am pretty good at it, too. I also like to make up children's stories and I have a few stories, that hopefully will become novels for me soon.

I love to fish and bird watch. I love smelling and feeling beautiful flowers and other flora.

I enjoy exploring cemeteries and graveyards. Finding the oldest grave is usually a goal or little game for me.

I love to find fossils and gemstones too.

Plus, I give pretty good advice, listen to those I care about, and love my fur babies like I gave birth to them.

I love giving personalized gifts, driving around enjoying nature, trying to imagine what the inside of each house looks like, and making others laugh.

I find that laughter has saved me and made me look a little crazy a few times (like when I laughed after being in a wreck), but I have an excellent sense of humor and am proud that it wasn't stifled during my childhood.

I love to laugh too. As a "latch key kid," and a "Gen Xer," I was raised on TV and movies. Movies and TV were everything. I have such a VAST knowledge of movies.

They are like dreams/nightmares come to life. I found out that I am and have always been more of a visual learner. Movies and TV became to me what a library (or bookstore) is to a bookworm.

Reading was not really encouraged in my home as a child. But I don't think that I would have read as many books as I have watched movies anyway. Of course, any movie that made me think interested me, but comedy was and is my favorite. Reading became a NEED as an adult. I LOVE to read now and do it often.

****

There has been so much laughter in my life. What a gift to have…

A baby's laugh may be the most beautiful sound in the whole world. It doesn't matter if a person has children or not, it is hard not to smile when it is heard.

Hearing each of my children's laughter as well as my husband's, brings so much pure joy to my life. I love to be the cause. Sometimes I do it intentionally and sometimes not at all. The best times are when they share their own sense of humor with me and we laugh together.

When I stop and think of all the laughter in my life, I feel like I waste too much time in my trauma and healing to realize how great my life has been since I met Theo. I have to start it there because that is truly when my real and true life began.

Moving out of "living in the past," should be a lot easier if I can focus on my life after I left home and became that newborn in the world. Time to stand on that bedrock of childhood and build a life of wonder.

****
**

Let's start with a question that most never think of.

What would I have been like as a child if all of my needs were met and I was free to just be me?

I would have put on beautiful girly dresses as often as possible, but especially in the summer, and explored the outdoors. I would have picked flowers after observing and smelling them. I would have done anything I could to make everything prettier or showcase the beauty of everything that I saw. I would have focused on art and music. I would have sung often with little made up songs in my head. I would have just loved being a very feminine girl. I would have loved to take dance lessons and just flit around everywhere I went.

I did like to play sports but it wasn't something that I would pick first. I loved fixing my hair and doing my make-up. I liked for everything to smell good too. And I KNOW that had I felt safe, I would have made everyone laugh with my quirky humor.

So why can't I be that now?

Well, who says that I can't?

Obviously, there are things that can be tweaked to fit into my adult life. But, all of those things are still attainable. Those are things that can be done wether or not I become supernatural. They are the foundation of me.

First, this path I am on is not based on a religion. Hopefully, what little I do mention about a God or "savior" will be the only time I reference religion. I want this process to be void of it.

It is time to believe in my now and future and no longer believe in my past, as Dr Dispenza recommends. It is the difference between living in survival mode and living in creative mode.

For me to start manifesting the future I will need to teach myself how to control my brain and the way it functions, starting with wavelength manipulation in the brain.

Of course there is science involved in the process. According to the doctor in this subject's study, we live in our stress by keeping our brains in what is known as Beta brain waves. The faster the Beta wave, the more in our stress we are.

There are Delta waves present while we sleep solidly. This is the lowest and slowest wave. Our Alpha waves happen when we let our mind drift while our body continues in its task. Beta waves cover our waking thoughts but are used in reaching our goal of reaching Gamma waves. It is a strange order.

You would think that it would go -(slowest to fastest wavelengths)

Delta
Theta
Alpha
Beta
Gamma

But to reach a meditative level to manifest and create it goes in a different order.

Delta
Alpha
Beta
Theta
Gamma

I need to figure out how to take my brain from a slow wave to fast to slow to super fast.

I understand the result of going into Alpha waves and sort of know how to get there. The others are still a mystery though.

Well, for now.

I am only half way through the television version of the method on how to become "supernatural."

CHAPTER 9

****

**

What makes me think that all of this is even possible?

I have learned that there are people in our world that have found and shared long lost information about our species and its evolution.

I have listened to and read Graham Hancock's amazing theories that say that our history is wrong. He is not the only person who has dedicated their lives to finding the truth. Do I believe him? Absolutely!

I find it upsetting and intriguing that there is so much for us still to discover and learn about.

From the legends lost to us in South America and Central America, to artifacts that somehow survived the, most of the time, brutal colonization by Europeans in history.

There, luckily, are many secrets that we (in our era) are just now discovering thanks to LiDAR technology which uses a pulsing light laser that measures distances on the Earth. There are also modern day archeologists discovering lost cultures. Thanks to the thick ground cover and over growth, the invaders didn't destroy it all.

I find it fascinating that our species seems to have been here FAR longer than previous science could prove. Our technology and methods of carbon dating are more advanced but, as discovery goes, there may be a better and more accurate way. Until someone stumbles upon the discovery, we have to trust in our own findings for our time.

It sounds scary when you think of it like that. What are we denying ourselves?

We also need to be aware of our folklore and old tales. There must be elements of truth in each of the tales that we've seen adapted to fit a certain society or culture.

The great flood, for instance. It is told and retold. It is adapted to fit the need of the people of the time. The story of its occurrence is told in all major religions that I know of,. not to mention that the scientific proof keeps adding up.

It is believed that a comet or meteor or some form of outer space object streaked across the skies over the northern continents after entering our atmosphere. It broke apart and fell over much of Europe, Scandinavia, Iceland, and Canada. When it did this over 12,600 years ago, our planet had a great amount of ice at its poles. These falling objects hit so fast and with such heat and power, it instantly melted the northern half of the Earth's ice. The evidence of how it happened in Canada can be seen in the Pacific North West near the Yellowstone area. This caused massive flooding. The waters washed away everything in its path.

EVERYTHING!

Now, imagine what would happen if that were in today's time. All settlements, people, flora and fauna were wiped out. The area around Turkey where most of the major religions started has many tales of the great flood. There is even one with a human that was said to have built an ark for the animals. I believe he could have known to prepare because of astronomy. If something like, let's say, Haley's Comet was expected to arrive in a certain year, and it was known to bring destruction, wouldn't you prepare? It would make more sense and be more realistic. When the waters started covering the Earth, where did all traces of humanity go? Who could survive such a thing without being prepared?

I believe that the flood did happen, but not the way it was explained and told to me. I love that science is now catching up with our ancient tales. I love that we feel that we are evolved enough to understand the how's and why's for the ancient tales. I get all of that. What I want to know, is where is the debris? Did it wash into our oceans? Would we find proof in our Great Lakes? Was it buried under mud left by the waters?

The way our glaciers scrape the Earth's surface clean when it moves should tell us a great deal. Is there proof in our ice caps frozen until it is released once thawed? I wonder these things. I know it would make sense if anything found from that event were discovered in these areas.

Why does this matter?

Well, for someone like me who wants to believe in magic and all things supernatural, having a bit science involved proves that what we know is not even a portion of what is left to discover. Not to mention, that along with the great flood story there are many people who have been known to perform "miracles" or "magic," in many of those folklore tales.

Why couldn't that be true for today?

Who is to say that a great civilization wasn't wiped off the globe by a great flood. I believe there is an old story about a place called Atlantis. But, we haven't found proof...yet. They were said to be extremely advanced. What is meant by that, I don't know. Advanced technologically or advanced by evolution? Could there have been people that can do many, if not all, that we imagine from these tales?

Why not? I am willing to try and figure out how it is possible. And hopefully I'll succeed.

I am willing to learn to raise my brain waves to be able to access the unknown genetic parts of myself that is said to be there. I am willing to try mind bending and natural drugs to see what these modern archeologists/scientists have discovered. I am willing to travel to remote locations that offer these mind opening and expanding experiences that seem to not only balance our brain's chemistry but can connect us to the path in our brains that lead to the higher consciousness that we should all have easy access to by the time we are adults. It should be a part of our upbringing. We have been cut off from our own possibilities. We have been trained to think that our life should be the ho-hum and dreary life that has been pushed on us from a system that has never worked for the people. The current system has only ever benefitted the wealthy or should I say the mega greedy.

When we all stop playing their game, we will be able to remake our world in the image it was meant to always be. We are a species on this planet. We aren't THE species. We are only one. We are the ones who are intelligent and sentient enough to know that we are the keepers of this world.

When did we forget that?

When did we stop loving our world? When did we forget our connection to it and that that connection is just as important as our connection to ourselves and our higher consciousness? One of the lessons that this world can teach us is compassion. This is especially true with animals. How a person reacts to, or treats, the creatures on this planet, reveals a great deal about their soul and their level of evolution in their consciousness.

CHAPTER 10

Chakra 6

****
**

How do I KNOW I am on the right track?

I have tried past life progression. I found a man
on youtube that recorded himself going
through it with a group. I found the process an
exercise in trust. Trusting myself to listen,
keep an open mind and take what came into
my mind as the message or vision of these
experiences. I have done this a few times
because I felt that I had more past lives to
discover.

This is what came through during the first one.

It was early in the day. I was walking. I looked
down and saw little sock covered feet in
sandals. Not normal sandals like I wear now but
ones that look like some type of wood with
two solid straps across my foot. I looked up
and found my hand in my mothers hand. I am

assuming it was my mother. That is the feeling I had. She was on the thin side with black hair that was pulled up and back but was not tight against her head. She was wearing a dress. It was a cream colored dress with a shimmer in places that gave it a design. All of a sudden everything went white. I was looking at a burst of light that made me disappear. I knew that I was gone for about five seconds and then I was really gone. It was the atomic bomb dropping in Japan and I was a toddler. Wow.

The second time I had a vision I was standing on a boulder in a very dry and sparse landscape. It looked like the desert in the South West. I looked at my feet. They were covered in a leather type boot that only came up a little above my ankle. I was also wearing pants made of a softer leather or canvas like material. The pants were a lighter shade than the shoes. They were almost the same color as the sand. The shoes were more like the red clay dirt color. I was a Native. My cousin or brother was standing on the ground in front of me. It was a drop of about six feet. The boulder cast a shadow. My cousin was walking softly, almost crouching, with his palms facing forward. I could see that he was approaching something or someone that must have been scared. All of a sudden something hit my back and made me fall forward. I landed in the sand below. I was part in the sun and part out. I could now see that there was a woman in a long black dress with light colored hair. She was screaming now. I couldn't move. I was paralyzed by the bullet wound in my back. Then men started to appear. They came toward me and then I was gone. I am not sure if they shot me again or if I just died.

I have also discovered that I was a bee and a bear. The bee was interesting. I got to fly. I felt an almost inhalation of air before I fly. It wasn't a breath in my lungs but under my body hairs. It tingled and helped me fly.

The bear was on a mountain outcropping or rocky hill that was the home of the cave I exited. I could feel my muscles. They were a bit sore and my feet felt really heavy. I had a bad headache. I could feel my anger and hunger. I guess I was hangry. I could smell everything. Every smell was potential food.

The latest life was probably the strangest because it wasn't human or an earthly creature. I was blue in color. I was a woman but I was half snake. My scales were not normal snake scales.(or how I picture them because...well... I don't think I have ever touched a snake... on purpose.) They looked more like what we picture for a dragon or more fish-like but were part of my skin. My partner was orange or similar to the red clay of earth. That is not all that is odd. I am "married" to a God. I feel the overwhelming acceptance, love and deeper connection. This is not my orange partner. This "God" was like nothing I had ever imagined or seen in this earthly life.

He was a huge oval of light. He was so bright that he formed a face in the center to lessen the glow. He had colors shooting out at the edges of what I could see of him. We had two sons. I know this. They are grown men. They each have brown skin like those that I have seen in the Middle East with dark hair and facial hair, but in different styles for each. Our existence was timeless.

I am in need of sexual pleasure. I felt the tingling and longing. But my GOD/husband was too powerful in his real form to have actual sex. He could transform into a human but preferred to stay in his light form. It is as if a glowing magic oval mirror is talking to me. I am aware that I am not his only wife or mate. There is no jealousy or animosity toward the others. That is not my business. It seems completely separate from our time together. I also feel that although we have sons, they were not made the usual way. Maybe they were in a non typical egg? Like a leather egg? I can't see the exact make-up, but I sense it. It is completely foreign to me.

Because my husband in this regression is of a higher consciousness, he made sure that I have a true love/soulmate that goes from life to life with me and fulfills me sexually and emotionally. My clay colored partner is an extension of me and my husband. He is part me (DNA) but brought to life by my husband. We are lovers in the purest way, me and my soul mate.

I get to feel and have all of the pleasures of the flesh AND be eternal. I have no idea what this creature is that I appear to be nor where it comes from.

The closest thing that I have found in the

information of the day (internet) is the creature called Naga/Nagini and African legends known as Mama/Mami Wata. I don't have the knowledge nor the experience to tell you what that means.

I found that Mami Wata has many lovers but she requires them to be faithful to only her. For whatever reason, this doesn't feel abnormal to me. I know our society tells us to be monogamous but each individual is different. Not everyone has the same needs, wants, or kinks, for lack of a better word. To find a partner, or partners, that feels the same way with the same interests, is such a rarity because most don't know what it is they actually want.

I would like to try the regression once more. Maybe it will reveal another aspect of my soul. The video I used can be found on Youtube.

(https://youtu.be/lKtEk8BDeo) Dr. Brian Weiss will lead you into the state of mind needed to regress comfortably.

Do I have Spirit Guides?

I have heard that we have guardian angels, spirit guides, and/or our ancestors that help guide us from another dimension. I followed an exercise found on the internet to connect with them. I asked my spirit guides for their names and a validation.

I heard "Sue." My family has many "Sue's." Was this just something familiar that popped into my mind or was her name actually, "Sue?" I asked for a validation. I felt that the validation would come through the television. I turned it on and the word that I noticed was "Song." The only person I know with that last name is a girl named "Su!" That was clear enough for me. I also had a girl named "Bianca" and a guy who had a nickname of "Bingo." I have also had many dreams with a guy named "Victor." Any and all that I feel are around me are welcome. Hopefully they can help me expand my mind. If this is the first step to be completely open to other dimensions, I am excited to feel the freedom and experience the journey.

What about Aliens?

I know that aliens must be real. There is definitely something out there.

I have seen a UFO with my own eyes. I saw it in Mississippi while riding in the car with one of my friends on the way home from community college. It was the middle of the day with not a cloud in the sky.

There it was...an oblong white oval just floating in the sky. As we acknowledged it, it shot across the sky. I was 18 at the time.

CHAPTER 11

****
*

Religion has no appeal to me. NONE. Some of the more damaging and dramatic incidents of my life involve religion.

My mother was a Catholic. Her father, my Grand-Daddy was from a family of mixed religion. His mother was Jewish and his Dad wasn't. My maternal Grandmother was born into a Catholic home. This is just to point out that there were conflicts of religion in my family for many generations. My parents didn't follow the same branch of Christianity either.

My mom met my dad when they were both in junior college. They ran off (eloped) and got married because mom was pregnant. My dad is Baptist. His dad, my Paw-Paw, was born in New Orleans and I want to say that he was Catholic. My Maw-Maw was Baptist.

Because of this, my mom took us (my older sister and me) to Catholic church alone, and as we entered the ages where we should be going through certain Catholic rituals, we fell behind. They wouldn't allow me to go into a children's class of my age group because it went by level of study. When my sister and I fell behind too much, we stopped going all together.

My mom met a woman at work whose husband was a Baptist preacher. She extended an invitation to the family to come check out their church. I am sure my mom was dismissive about giving up her Sunday for Baptist church so the coworker asked if she could possibly come get us (the kids) to join her at her church on Sunday mornings. This kind woman had kids our age and knew that it would make us more comfortable. This became a regular thing. Why wouldn't we want to escape our home for a few hours?

When my parents saw how happy it made us, they wanted to be a part of it. That is when church became a status thing to them both. Church became another stage for my mother and another way for my dad to get away from her and us.

Sundays were torture. We would get cussed

out, yelled at, forced to dress up and were told
to not embarrass them. Then we would step
out of our van and act like we lived in some
fairytale. All of the freedom to be and learn
was gone. Church was just another place that
we had to survive. After, we'd go home and be
put to work. Our whole Sunday afternoon was
usually a cleaning day unless my mom or dad
invited someone over; then the theatrics
continued. The Jekyll and Hyde version of my
mom wasn't new. We just had more rules to
follow.

Learning about some almighty entity that can,
at random, make your life better or worse, is
strange when you live in a hellscape. Where
was his protection? Didn't he love children? If
he is so powerful, why is life this way for me
and my siblings? Obviously, I would have to
look at these stories of his life and miracles
from a different angle. I had to look at his
humanity, not supposed divinity. It would have
to be absorbed like a history lesson, benign to
my life. They would just be fables of a time
past...nothing more. The lifestyle that was
expected from all of his followers was clearly
translated incorrectly. I doubt such a pure soul
would agree with the way religion is

misrepresenting his message and life. Religion's societal parameters make it nearly impossible for regular people to live the right way. There were very few people in the church that set the example. (Ms Audrey was one that did.)

When I stopped going to church, it was a relief to my soul. It was the same freedom I felt when I got off of Facebook. Neither one was furthering my growth as a human.

As a moldable teen, any feelings of distrust, embarrassment or hurt can forever taint a memory of not just people but places too. Once again, mom made sure to mark her stage.

While attending the church of her coworker, my mom decided that she and my dad should renew their vows. I want to say it was for their 13th wedding anniversary. My mom had all of her children in the ceremony...except for me, the scapegoat. My older sister was a bridesmaid. My baby sister was the flower girl. My brother was a groomsman and walked my mom down the aisle. My baby brother was the ring bearer. I could have been the other bridesmaid, but my mom chose a lady that she had never talked about from work. She made me sit at the door to make everyone sign the guestbook. Until recently I thought that was the worst of it. Then I realized that she wanted everyone to see that I was not in the wedding. I had to present a good face like it didn't crush me. But it did. I wanted to cry the whole time. Did she know that it hurt my feelings so much? Probably. Did she care? Not AT ALL.

When that small church didn't bring her enough status, she moved us to a larger church. This kept her busy, thankfully. It also gave me and my siblings more friends to be around. The youth group was amazing. I made some of my lifelong friends there.

Being a member of this church allowed us to travel. The youth group occasionally took a fun trip. This wasn't one of those "mission trips" where you had to share a religious message to some random people that didn't need nor want the message. We were going to Panama City Beach, Florida. It would be the first trip without my parents. Of course I wanted to go.

My mom decided that if I wanted to go, I had to earn the money. It was something like $300 or so, to go. I thought about it and decided to call my Maw-Maw and ask if I could earn some money by cleaning her house during the summer. She lovingly agreed.

She knew what it was for and how much I wanted to go. I worked every week to earn my funds. My Maw-Maw and I timed it out so that I would have enough earned in time to go. When the week of the trip arrived, I was packed. I had bought a new swimsuit with my own money and got everything I needed too. Two days before the trip, My mom decided that my older sister could go. She had had other obligations over the summer and knew that it wouldn't be possible for her. But she saw how happy I was and wanted to go too.

My mom and dad forked out the cash for her, no questions asked, no stipulations, no working all summer. She got to go for free. It was upsetting but I wasn't going to let that spoil my trip.

When we got to Florida, we had so much fun. I actually had my one an only summer romance while there. This sweet young man from Albany, Georgia, took a liking to me. I had

never had a guy show me attention. I was
never a first choice. He wanted to be around
ME. He was very sweet and not bad looking
either. His family made candy canes; that was
their family's business. They were staying in a
summer rental on the beach. His name was
Don B.

Yes, I still remember his full name. He made me
feel beautiful for the first time in my teenage
years.

Even when I woke one morning with sun
poisoning on my face. My lips and face had
swollen during the night and I couldn't even
keep spit in my mouth. Luckily, one of the
chaperones was a nurse and knew how to help.
Once the swelling mostly went down, I
constantly had zinc sunblock all over my face. I
looked ridiculous.

But Don still saw me as beautiful. How could I
forget him? He chose to like me over all of the
girls on the trip. We spent time together. It
was so very innocent. We went sailing.

We went to the local amusement park and he
introduced me to Beastie Boys ("No Sleep till

Brooklyn"). I introduced him to LL Cool J. ("I Need Love").

We went swimming and kissed.

That is it.

It was so sweet and appropriate for a summer romance. This was the summer before my sophomore year in high school.

It was an amazing trip for me.

My sister bought Puka shell necklaces for my siblings and little things for my parents. I mean... They DID give her the money. She should be thankful. I got them some postcards in place of pictures to show them what everything looked like. They were cheaper than buying a camera and waiting for the film to be developed. Plus, they were better pictures than I could take. I wanted them to see how beautiful it was.

When we returned to the church, on arrival, one of the youth ministers who was on good terms with my parents told my mom in a joking way, "You need to get that one checked for AIDS!" ... talking about me. It was a kick in the gut. That was not funny at all. This was in the mid 1980's. My mother looked at me with hate in her eyes. Oh, I would pay for this!

When we finally got home and my sister started handing out gifts, my mom asked where mine were. My what? Gifts? No. I didn't buy gifts. This was a trip I EARNED. My sister didn't.

I pulled out my postcards to show them what it looked like. I got belittled and hit for being so "selfish." It was just another of her "rules," that I should have expected.

There are so many stories like this in my life. SO much abuse, manipulation, deceit, and favoritism.

One clear display was when my sister was bought a used car her senior year as a graduation present. I got luggage and had to beg to go see a dentist for the first time. That was my graduation present. Yes, I was grateful for the gifts.

I also had to deal with racism. In high school, my friends couldn't come over if they were black. I heard, "Where are they going to brush their hair?" Yet, my (black) friend's mom was SO welcoming to me. I stayed over, helped them clean in the morning, (I was part of the family) and felt nothing but acceptance.

It would be years and would take until my youngest brother had friends of a different skin color and wanted to visit, before this rule in my home changed.

I know. Just one more thing I had to fight against. I refused to teach this type of thinking to my own children and refused to have any part in racist behavior.

Funnily enough, I have never heard a racist remark come out of my dad's mouth, just from my mom. But as it turns out, she is the most diverse genetically of everyone in my family! This includes some African ancestry. Actually, both of my parents passed down some African ancestry. I have had everyone's DNA tested in my family and also the grandparents. I am working on my siblings next.

I am not sure to this day if she still feels this way toward people of a different color. I don't

really want to know. It is not my karma or
negativity.

CHAPTER 12

****
**

What if your abuser plays the long game?

Until recently, I didn't realize just how much my mom must have hated me as a teen. Like I mentioned before, I love the arts. I jumped at any chance to take part. I sang and got involved in plays and puppeteering in church because my small country school didn't even have a chorus at that time. There were no art classes, no drama, no dancing…all the things I loved. But they did have band classes, which I had dedicated myself to since 6th grade. I played the clarinet. They only had basic sports at first, like football, basketball, track and baseball. I believe there was only basketball and track for girls.

My school gained a girls' softball team my sophomore year, and the very first dance team came my senior year. Of course, I had to be a part of it. Even though I had not been blessed to be in a family that could afford to take dance lessons, I could see a dance move and do it eventually. It just took practice. I made the team and even though I wasn't the first choice, I got to be an officer. That meant that I got to lead. This was the first time for me. I got to teach my own set of underclassmen during practice while the other officers taught their group. It was what my soul needed. I had never been given this honor before. I loved it.

When it came time to apply to college. I chose the local community college. I wanted my freedom and education. I tried out for the dance team, show choir and band. I made all three and then some. I had five scholarships in all. My college cost was under $800 for the year. I applied for loans but couldn't get any in my name because my parents still claimed me on their taxes. It is just how the system worked. Well, because of this, my parents took out a small loan to cover the cost and to give me a little spending money/allowance each week ($20).

I loved college. Just loved it! I wasn't the best student but I passed or failed in my semi-free world with contentment. I knew I could fix my grades. I needed to figure out my own system to make it all work with all of my extra curricular (scholarship) activities.

Of course, when it came time to go back in the fall of my second year, I couldn't wait. I had my dance team gear for practices and had gone to one practice when I was informed, by my parents, that if I wanted to go back to college, I needed to get a job! Now, that is not a big deal. I could get a job. But, I had no car and only a month to make $800. The college required you to stay on campus so a job would not be possible once school started.

I tried. I tried so hard. I got a job at the local Walmart for $4.25 and hour. When the first paycheck came, I knew that there was no way for me to achieve my goal.

I had to give up my scholarships. I had to do it in enough time to allow the new girl that took my place (and scholarships) time to adjust to her windfall.

My heart was broken. All I wanted to do was leave. That is when I decided to join the Air Force.

I found out years later why all of this took place.

After I had had my children, exited the Air Force, and was home for a visit, my mom told me in private (always in private) that she had been jealous of me. She told me that when she was in college, she tried out for the show choir but only made the chorus. She also told me that she had always wanted to join the military. She had been jealous that I got to do what she wanted.

It is remarkable that she could even recognize the emotion of jealousy in herself. But the fact that she knew she had been that way during it all and was letting me know, in private, that she had that kind of power over me, made me feel sick to my stomach.

As I am going through therapy and am figuring out the wounds done to my soul, I am looking at things through new eyes. I see now why my parents did what they did. Apparently, my life looked too good. I was too happy. During this year of manipulation was when the whole "moving out" thing happened.

How and why would a parent ever be jealous of their child? It is my understanding that as a parent, a goal is to give my children more and better than I had. I don't understand the jealous mind set. It is a narcissistic mind set. The fact that she made sure to never mention this around my siblings says a lot.

My siblings told me years ago that my mom wrote them apology letters. Well, just to the siblings who got physically beat like me. But, she apologized...to them. I didn't receive a letter. I know why too. It comes down to the fact that I am still the scapegoat.

She told my siblings that she gave me a letter, but she didn't. Why would she tell them this? Because if I bring up our childhood with my siblings, they wonder why I can't let it go. Why don't I accept her apology and see that she has changed? Because I know she hasn't.

It is part of that whole, "Make her out to be crazy" plan, or into someone who can't stop talking bad about our mom's actions from our childhood.

I know this now. I know that my siblings KNOW

what actually happened. I just worry that she has really brainwashed them to not see her continued narcissism techniques. I don't blame them if they can't see. It should be obvious at this point but maybe they don't want to or aren't ready to accept their trauma.

When my siblings and I started having children, favoritism became a thorn in our sides. Our mom started showing favoritism to certain grandchildren. This "stirred the shit" in the family. My mom was trying to get us to fight for her attention and "love."

I never worried about that because I didn't really want her techniques used on my children.

She ignored them equally.

That is the closest my mom ever got to being truly fair. My dad has spent even less time with my kids throughout their childhood than my mom. My parents are textbook.

Oh, my kids have seen her mask fall enough to know that what I say is true. They have seen the true face of their "Nana" and the dismissive, and enabling ways of my dad.

I don't have to worry about that on my husband's side of the family. It is always fair when it comes to my children. My children are loved and know it.

It has taken me many years to come to this level of realization about the events of my childhood and the reason behind my mother and all that she did and still does.

I don't know what makes a narcissist. Is it by birth or do they become in their environment? Of course, no matter the reason, there is no excusing child abuse.

I try to think of why my mom has formed this over-inflated sense of importance or why she thinks that she is better than everyone else. Looking at her life on the surface, it is not expected. My mom is a twin. She was born second and was unexpected.

In a normal situation, she should have been the child vying for attention in a large family. But my grandparents had a daughter a little over a year before "the twins" were born.

That baby girl was premature at birth. She was born in New Mexico in the mid-1900's. Medical technology was not what it is today. This beautiful little girl was given too much oxygen in her incubator which resulted in extreme brain damage. She grew up to have the mental capacity of an eight year old or younger. She needed special care her whole life, as well. She lived in a home that took care of her in her adult years but as a child she was home.

When my mom was born a surprise, my grandmother and grandfather thought she was some miracle replacement baby for the damaged one. Her whole life she was hyped up and told that she was more special than the other children, even her twin, even though they are identical. (They like to say that they aren't, but, in the very next breath will say that they are in fact "mirror twins." Time has shown that that means they are in fact, identical...physically.) My poor aunt (her twin) must have felt resentful. I can't tell you if my aunt is also a narcissist because I don't know her like I do my own mother.

I did end up telling my mom's twin about the abuse a couple of years ago. She was shocked.

She told me that she always felt like something was off with mine and my mom's relationship. My aunt wishfully told me that I should have been her daughter because we share more interests than my mother and I do.

But I wasn't meant to be her daughter.

I would like to think that as my (Catholic) godmother, I could have counted on her for her support if I had not been so scared of my mother as a child, and most of my adult years.

As my mom's twin, I know that would have been difficult. My abuser is a master manipulator. She can look you in the eye and deny, lie, twist a story and make herself look like a victim.

The problem with all of her woes is that she is trying to look like a victim during a time when she had all of the power. I have never witnessed such a thing.

She acts like her smallest and weakest child (physically) was the cause of all of that rage that she couldn't control against her children.

BUT I now know.

None of her acts were my fault. I can walk away from that time with my head held high. I survived! I can still be me. I can still become everything that I always wanted to be.

I am not talking about being a ballerina, or an archeologist like Indiana Jones. I am talking about the true, deep down, happy, loving, giving, silly, sarcastic, creative, intelligent, talented and absolutely beautiful soul that I know I am and have always been. No more fear to...BE! I can rise above and become and so can anyone else.

Including my mom!

Yes, I believe that if she went to therapy for many years, sincerely apologized, and could truly raise her consciousness, she too could be a good person. But first, she would have to accept that she has done wrong and is still doing it.

She would have to raise her frequency to match mine. Otherwise, I will not entertain her company. I can not allow her presence in my life, but that is just the way it has to be.

To be honest, I will not allow her in my new life regardless if she is actually able to change. I have stopped expecting things to be different with her. It is my choice to end familial contact with my mother.

CHAPTER 13

****
**

I had to stop my big beautiful heart from wasting energy hoping that I am wrong about her and she isn't... she doesn't mean to....

But, what if my mom has already changed for the better?

What if she did her changing while i've been away discovering my own path?

After so much personal reflection and guidance from my former therapist, Alyssa, and my absolutely amazing current therapist, Katie, I now see the actions and my responses to being raised by a narcissist/enabler are part of the conditioning that resulted from my traumatic upbringing.

I had a moment in my growth where my heart's longing slipped through. I had a moment of doubt. I almost stopped writing all of this. I thought about how nice my mom has been to me in the last three years, or so. I had a moment that I questioned wether I was being fair to her... Then I came to my senses. If my mother was really a changed "Christian" woman who truly practiced what she preached, I would not have been made aware of her most recent attempts to hurt me. (I use this perimeter to justify her deliberate actions because that is how SHE describes herself. Religion is not something I choose to be a part of.)

Anyone who is living in their victimhood, or survival mode, can, and should, become aware of their environment and their position in it. It is only then that they can start to regain their own power and become the person that they were always meant to be. It is (and would be) a tragedy to lose that unique individual that may have been meant for great acts benefitting humanity.

I know that for a person who experienced any physical abuse, damage to the body and any resulting marks are obvious to the abused. Marks are undeniable. But, the mind games of abusers can be subtle and not so subtle at times. These are some of the acts that I am aware of by my abuser:

I have asked my family and friends to not call me a certain nickname. It made me feel like I did growing up. I only find it comforting or acceptable from my nieces and nephews, who call me the nickname but they put "Aunt" in front. It is so sweet. The name otherwise is so bland. It makes me think of a useless blob. Don't ask me why. And guess who ONLY calls me that nickname now? Yep…you can probably guess.

—————————————————————————————————————

My mom made a point, on social media, to praise my son when he was in the Navy like he was her child, and also mentioned my husband who served in the Army for Veterans' Day. That is all.

Okay, so she is proud of her grandson (who was active duty at the time and not yet a veteran) and son-in-law. That would be okay if I wasn't proud of my time in the USAF. I got a bit triggered. She knew which buttons to push.

Yes, It is petty.

So she did not mention my service. So what! I Know! That is why it ticked me off.

She loves to push the buttons that she created.

I called her on it and she didn't like it. She went around telling all of our local family that I overreacted and was ridiculous over it.

Granted, I did get upset, but, I never physically showed it to her. I live many states away from her. She knew she upset me because I reacted. That was her goal.

I fell for it. I was weaker then.

____
—

My abuser made sure that my favorite aunt did not include me in her wedding. My aunt informed me that when she finally found the love of her life a few years ago and became engaged, my abuser came up to her with demands.

She tried to dictate to her and delusionally demanded, "You better not just invite her(me) to your wedding. You better invite the rest of my kids too." This is what my aunt told me.

My aunt rightfully became defensive. My aunt made sure that NO ONE from my family was invited. I think that was justified. I truly don't blame her.

When my aunt told me why she didn't invite me, she was ashamed. I made sure she knew that she did the right thing. She stood her ground. Unfortunately, it had the desired effect that my mother/abuser wanted.

I didn't know until a couple of months after my aunt was married that she even found her guy, much less married him.

Funnily enough, it was my abuser that told me she got married. Huh, I wonder why that is? She wanted my authentic reaction to my favorite aunt not including me. The conniving way that came about was her narcissistic dream come true.

Unfortunately for her it only brought my aunt and me closer together. My aunt is aware of my abuser, her abusive past, as well as her brother's complacency to the whole situation. I made her aware.

Side note: My aunt had her closest brother and his wife at her wedding. It was a pretty ceremony. She is truly loved as she should be. She waited a very long time to find my new uncle. I am extremely happy for her.

————————————————————————————————

My aunt also gave me her piano. She sold my grandparents' home and downsized with her new husband. She knew that I was the most musical in the family. She knew how many good memories I had of my grandparents and her because of it. She even rented a trailer to drive it from the Gulf Coast area to my current state of Maryland. It was a lovely little visit. She and my new uncle could only stay for 2 days so there really wasn't a lot of time for sightseeing. But, we enjoyed each other's company. That is all I could ever want. I would have been just as happy if she didn't have a gift in tow.

I wanted to cry. She overwhelmed me with the

honor of the gift.

I love that piano... every out of tune note, every ding and scratch.

I see my grandmother (Maw-Maw) sitting at it playing and singing Christmas tunes. She always put her country or bluesy spin on the trills. She had such joy on her face when she played.

Of course, this didn't sit well with my mom. She tried to get my aunt to give it to one of my siblings instead of me. Why? Is that even a mystery?

I know why. I pay attention to the patterns and now know what drives her.

It may seem that I am hyper-focused on her actions. That is because I am. I have to be on guard every second she is in my life.

I refuse to participate in her manipulation. I will never fall victim again, if I can help it.

————————————————————————————
—

My abuser has told new members of the family that I am the different one. In 2020, a family member let me know that my name was brought up at a family gathering. This person said that my mom was sitting around a dinner table when this was said…

"She is the way she is by her choice! She feels that everyone is against her, and really it's her just choosing to separate because her beliefs are indifferent…." Then summarized the rest. "Your mom mentioned your kids, and how you allow them to do as they please without judgement and consequence, and that is why they are the way they are… but she made sure to end it with, she loves you all."

When my loved one told me that my mom had said this, my first reaction was like a Momma Bear. All I wanted to do was tell her off for suggesting that my kids are somehow lesser. Then I took a breath.

I was puzzled about what my mother meant at first. Then I realized that she must have been telling others, through standard narcissists manipulation, that I am not a real "Christian."

I am actually not a "Christian" the way she measures it, thankfully.

I am sure she has said things like, "She makes up stories about things that never happened," or "...exaggerated versions of things that did happen." It sounds like something she'd say.

For whatever reason, my narcissist abuser acts like she is in competition with me. She acts like MY life, happiness, successes, and appearance in the world is somehow a threat to hers.

I am not in competition with her and never have been. Therefore her view is askew.

I actually don't want her anywhere near my life.

My "versions" of things are not versions. They are truths....LONG hidden truths.

So, If I never see or hear from her again, it would be a painful yet bittersweet blessing. She IS my mother after all. She should be someone I WANT in my life.

I always have had a hope that one day she will truly change, but that is a beautiful dream that will have to live only in that dreamworld. My heart wants so much FOR her but my brain knows that she is limited by her mental issues. She will always be looking for a way to victimize the people around her to make her life more grandiose.

Luckily for all of her future victims, she can't physically abuse them. She doesn't have the power she had when her children were living under her roof. I hope my dad doesn't end up needing specialized care in his late years. I can only imagine how she would treat him.

Side note:

You know, my childhood had many good memories too. There are even many good ones with my abuser. Trips to the mall and having yummy waffle cone sundaes, watching movies together (Laughing at 1982's Poltergeist together to the point of almost peeing ourselves.) I look back and remember a good bit of laughter and what I thought was love.

My siblings played such a big role in forming my personality. They were also my saviors. They helped me see that I was cared for in ways my mom surely didn't know about. After being physically beat, sometimes my siblings would gather around me on my bed and hug me while I cried. It happened more times than I want to remember. They showed me what love really meant. In that type of environment, knowing that you aren't alone is a bittersweet comfort.

My siblings are not to blame for even the tiniest part in, or reactions to, our upbringing. Each had their own role to play in our abuser's world. The oldest three kids received the actual physical beatings.

My baby sister was so quiet and smart. She would observe and learn how to "be good" so she never received physical abuse. She knew how to stay out of sight.

My baby brother was...the baby. We protected him. He grew up free. My mom didn't include him in her games, luckily. He was our comic relief as well. He could make my mom laugh and snap out of one of her rages with one phrase.

"I love you, Momma."

I bet he has told her that more than the rest of us combined.

I am the only one of us that moved away. I am the fortunate one there.

I have had the opportunity to get the help I've needed to deal with my trauma.

They have had to deal with their own life paths while being in constant contact with their abuser.

It makes me want to cry for them.

No matter how my siblings feel about my revelations, I will always love them. They don't know how much they saved me. Had they not loved me, I don't think I would have survived our childhood. Their love was the strength behind my will. And man, did I have a strong will to live, or more appropriately, to survive. Once I knew that my abuser was the abnormal one, I knew I had to make it through.

I wanted to just be free.

But, being physically free didn't mean that I was mentally free.

I still have to heal my inner child. I also have to face my own demons head on. I have to fight for my life. I have to overcome the struggle to become me.

There is no easy path for anyone.

There is no way I can evolve without unzipping the coat of "victimhood."

Am I still expecting the coldness of abuse and the resulting responses?

I will never feel the warmth of my own soul's path if I am living in my own winter.

That means that I MUST remove the source of cold. I will remove myself from interacting with the source as well. This is just double protection for any progress I make in evolving.

I have come to look at my lessons in life that way. Each is a suit/coat that can be unzipped and stepped out of, to reveal a little more of the real me.

CHAPTER 14

****
**

There have been many steps along this path to
awakening....

According to my DNA, I am a product of the
WORLD. That is how I look at my results of the
break down of my ancestry.

Thanks to all of the genealogy sites, I have
found traces of ancestors from different
regions and many continents. It may not seem
important to some, but to me, it gives me a
leap-frog jump over my parents and
grandparents to discover who contributed to
the genetic makeup of me.

Why does this mean something to me?
Because, I get to have roots without emotion.
In researching the area and cultures, I get to
choose what I want and don't want by means
of traditions as well as beliefs and incorporate
them into my new personality, if it speaks to
me.

I love discovering their names as well as finding

stories or pictures of these ancestors. I get to build my family influences by choice, so to speak. Of course they came before me so their influence isn't so much felt as honored. I want to think that they would have loved me and welcome my inclusion.

My DNA breakup is as follows (From 23andme and AncestryDNA):

<u>(23andMe)</u>

Scotland, UK, & Ireland} 52.5%

Italy}13.3%

Ashkenazi Jew} 9.0%

Slovenia, Serbia, Kosovo, Romania, Moldova, Bulgaria, & Albania} 4.8%

Spain & Portugal} 2.6%

Sub-Saharan Africa} 1.2%

Indigenous American} .9%

Central Asia, Northern India, & Pakistan} .5%

Broad South Africa} .2%

<u>(ANCESTRY)</u>

England & Northwestern Europe} 40%

Scotland} 22%

Northern Italy} 9%

European Jewish} 9%

Wales} 9%

Ireland} 5%

Germanic Europe: Austria, Belgium, Czechia, Denmark, Hungary, Luxembourg, Netherlands, Slovakia, Slovenia, Switzerland} 2%

Basque} 1%

Indigenous Americas-North} 1%

Ivory Coast & Ghana} 1%

Benin & Togo} 1%

I love that there is such diversity in my blood. I feel a connection to each of my ancestral continents, countries/regions. What a blessing and treat to research their histories and many cultures.

Because I have been researching my family tree for over 20 years, I have found lines that lead back to many of the "DNA" areas. I have also found links to most of European royalty. It is easy once you find a link to a man or a woman with Sir or Lady in front of their name. The records are even on wikipedia.

I have found a link to a female African slave that I am 80% sure is in my line. I can't be 100% because of lack of records and written history of the African people. She would be one of my great grandmothers. She is linked to the Senegal area. I say area because I am not sure if that is where she was from or if that is where she was sold into slavery and transported. It is heartbreaking to know this happened to her. She makes me proud, which is not always the case when I discover ancestors.

It is really unnerving to descend from oppressors as well as the oppressed. It makes me feel the burden of the generational wounds that must be healed. But I have a lot of pride in them all. They lived their lives, learned their lessons and passed them on to their offspring in hopes that they not be forgotten. I "see" all of them as part of me!

There are many farmers, blacksmiths, welders, preachers, chauffeurs, merchants, fishermen, tailors, home makers, soldiers (military), servants and many more. (This is found on census records.)

My favorite discoveries are the ones where you see a little of their personality, though.

I have a grandmother that told off a bunch of

church folk when they tried to enter her house to excommunicate my grandfather (her husband) for drinking on a Sunday. The record said that she spoke to them in a very "unchristian like manner,"or something to that affect. That made me smile.

Then I have a grandfather that was punished for helping natives escape the encroaching French army. He was one of the last people to be "broken on the wheel" in our country. That made me sad and proud.

Obviously, there is nothing I can do to change the past. It is what it is. A locked in, yet mirage like, history. How much is true and accurate can sometimes change to half truths or complete lies. So I look at them like such. The more I study and research our history, the more that I am aware of the one-sided view that we all have been taught. Every story in our history has two sides and rarely, if ever, is the side of the loser or oppressed told.

Strangely, It isn't just our country's history, it is world wide. The "truth" about many things have been kept from the public. The more I learn, the less I trust written history. Recent archeological finds and geological finds tell different stories from the ones we have been taught. There is even a difference in the stories in reference books. I own an old Encyclopedia Brittanica set that I bought second hand. It is different from the Encyclopedia Americana of the same time frame. That is just infuriating to me. Truth is truth. There should not be versions.

Once I started realizing that this was the case, the quest of finding the real me seemed even more open. By that I mean, I can be not just authentically me but I get to reeducate myself on the world's history. I get to fill my mind with truths that can be the basis of my personality.

****
*

The episodes of the show with the great Doctor are intense! They are not a quick watch. Each episode became a checkpoint. Some messages are easier to grasp than others. There is an episode that he talks about how test subjects spent four days training their minds to be in the positive 'now' instead of the negative 'past'.

I had to repeat this step a couple of times. I still have to perfect this technique. I am human after all. I make mistakes and learn lessons.

Isn't that why we are here in this time, in this consciousness, and on this journey called life?

After the first four day span with many failures and restarts, mind you, I had a lightened energy in my mind. I felt brighter....happier. I also noticed when someone around me was being negative. It was almost like someone had given me a magnifying glass to see the world. I began seeing more of my environment in my mind's eye. I was more aware of the energy in a room. I wanted to be alone much more.

How would I be able to get to the place of awareness of my own actions, if I was constantly examining everyone around me? Isolation seemed like the logical choice. So, I became somewhat of a hermit in my home.

I didn't watch an episode of "Rewired" every day. I needed to spend time with myself. I needed to get over myself and become what and who I was always meant to be.

I have seen many avenues and different paths that teach and lead to the same awakening of consciousness. Some are inside religions. Parts are shown in methods of meditation. Tantric sex, Kundalini, Ayahuasca rituals, legal Psilocybin micro-doses, and other means can give you a look into our own minds in a way that is, well, supernatural. No matter the path, we don't shake our demons until we have dealt with them. There is no other way and it isn't an easy road. Emotions will find a way to be dealt with.

Unfortunately, it is unavoidable. Trying to stop the emotional volcano from reaching a head when we face our past mistakes and traumas will only last for so long. Eventually, we will explode no matter if we are truly trying to change for the better.

I know I did. My volcano erupted in many ways and in many intensities. I have had more emotional outbursts in the last few months than I have probably had in ten years.

I have had to listen to my inner child. My sweet

inner child. She is a part of every decision I make. Does it please her or make her feel loved? If not, why not? What needs to be changed? What is acceptable and what is not? It is all very important. I don't put her first. I put her "equal." I include my body and higher self in every decision now.

But, my inner child is a remarkable, brave, strong willed and pure hearted part of me that has earned her right to rest and feel safe and loved.

I wish that she had been mine to raise. That sweet little girl would have been protected and cherished like she was meant to be.

She is mine now. She is and will forever be safe with me. I will never let anyone hurt her again. Never!

****

*

CHAPTER 15

I don't claim to be a doctor or even a pro at anything...yet. I am just a woman who has been in and out of college many times. I have 5.5 colleges under my belt. (.5 is the Community College of the Air Force because it was just part of my service if I participated) and have studied many things. If combined, I may have enough credits for a masters degree.

Unfortunately, a college degree wasn't meant for me (yet?). I can see why. I never would have been able to connect all of these clues and patterns if I had forced myself down a single minded career path. (For example, medicine, military, geology, law, math, the arts, science, etc.) I consider myself an autodidact of....everything! From the smallest of viruses and things like CRISPR all the way to what we believe to be the 5th dimension and time travel, and everything (and every being) in between.

I have read books and watched so many shows

on so many subjects. I have read everything from books on myths and folklore, quantum physics and everything in between. I have studied the history of our DNA and genetic manipulation. I have seen signs of ancient ruins, and the vast hidden history of our planet. I have watched numerous documentaries about the Earth and its evolution. I have learned about so many topics in science too.

I believe it all started by watching nature shows as a child, when Mutual of Omaha's Wild Kingdom was the best pick from all four available channels on TV.

I have learned about many animals and plants that have come and gone throughout our planet's history as well.

I have learned and read about everything from a single cell's mitosis to the universal codes for manifestation. Binary code with Fibonacci sequenced. Not to mention the inclusion of sound, vibration, frequency, and the elements. I am still working it out.

There are many things that I am using to

continue to learn who I am and how to trust my own intuition. I have a few sets of Tarot cards. I am drawn to my oracle/angel cards and my angel cards. They are more positive than the regular tarot. They also seem more personal. I write down which cards are drawn every day and what they mean to me. Hopefully, If I become proficient at listening to my intuition and at reading them, I can help others to listen to their own inner voices in whatever manner, medium, instrument, or material they choose. Trusting that intuition and listening to our bodies is what is missing for most people.

I also have books, not yet read, that talk about how to reach the 5th dimension. I have watched every show that has popped up that pertains to my journey and the methods that are leading me to greatness.

I say that like I am not already great. We all are. We just need to realize not only our worth in this world, but the impact that we can make on it. We also need to realize our worth to ourselves and how every thought leaves an impact on our soul's vehicle; our body.

I am going to continue meditating. I like to do it in a hot epson salt bubble bath with a box fan going to keep me cool. It is a two-fold benefit for me. First, I learned that a long hot bath can be the equivalent of a two mile brisk walk. I have joint problems at the moment so it is very difficult to sit with my knees in one position like what is required for yoga. Second, this helps me relax. It seems more productive for me to mix the elements of water, fire(heated), Earth (salt), and air (fan).

I have been studying Chakras and what can cause them to be blocked. There are seven energy points in the body that must be focused on to reach the ultimate goal. Most people don't know how connected yet separate our bodies are from our conscious minds.

I listen to certain frequency tones while in the tub and when I am sleeping. I also listen to songs that have helped me through this journey. I have noticed that I only I want to listen to songs that keep my energies where I like them. There are many songs and certain movies that I have no interest in watching or listening to anymore. They make me feel less than positive and that has become unacceptable to the new me. That doesn't mean that I am all "rated G". That is a societal moral parameter. If it makes me feel positivity, love, or joy, I like it! Period!

From Music, To Elevation of Frequency

song-artist

Breakaway -Kelly Clarkson (1,2,3)

Unwritten- Natasha Beddingfield (2&5)

I Don't Want To Be- Gavin DeGraw(3&6)

You and Me- Lifehouse (3,4,5)

Hallelujah- Pentatonix (3,4,5,6,7)

Wonderful- Everclear (1,3,4,5)

In My Blood- Shawn Mendes (1,3,4,5)

Bad Day- Daniel Powter (4&6)

Through Heaven's Eyes- Brian Stokes Mitchell(Prince of Egypt Soundtrack)(3,6,7)

Without you- David Guetta (feat. Usher)(1,4,7)

Fly- Nicki Minaj, Rihanna (2,3,6,7)

The Reason- Hoobastank (2,3,4)

Keep Your Eyes Open- NeedToBreathe (2,3,5,6,7)

Heroes- Zayde Wolf (2,3,5,6,7)

Best Day of My Life- American Aurthors (3,5,7)

Immortals- Fall Out Boy (2,5,6,7)

Stutter- Marianas Trench (2,3,5,6)

Dare You To Move- Switchfoot (1,4,6)

I2I- Tevin Campbell(The Goofy Movie Soundtrack)(2,4,6)

God is a Woman- Ariana Grande (2&4)

Got It In You- Banners (1&3)

Believer- Imagine Dragons (2,3,6,7)

Right Now- Van Halen (1-7)

Welcome To The Black Parade- My Chemical Romance (3,4,5,6)

Life is a Highway- Rascal Flats (1-7)

Human- Christina Perri (1,2,3,5)

Strangers Like Me- Phil Collins(Tarzan Soundtrack) (1,3,6)**

Right Here Right Now-Jesus Jones(1,6,7)

Am I Wrong- Nico & Vinz (1,2,3)

Burn It All Down-League of Legends,
PVRIS(1-7)

Hand In My Pocket- Alanis Morissette(1&3)***

Meant to Live- Switchfoot(6&7)

Keep Holding On- Avril Lavigne(YOU CAN DO
IT)

****

Each song resonated with me in different ways
and for different issues. Music has always been
a huge part of my life. It was my therapy and
escape when I had no other method of working
through my emotions.

What a gift that we have a whole music
industry where we have the unlimited creative
works of so many different people,
personalities, and emotions to draw from.

Each song resonated with different energy
centers in my body.

I progressed from the beginnings of
recognition and resonance of the message of

the song, to feeling a personal connection.

From working through the shadow work of that feeling and energy, to healing the pain and darkness of each energy point so that it opens to give and receive freely.

Each Chakra or energy point has a key that helped me pinpoint which emotion or reaction I felt while feeling the song in my soul.

For a quick Chakra reference:

1. The Root - "I am"

2. The Sacral Plexus- "I feel"

3. The Solar Plexus- "I can"

4. The Heart- "I love"

5. The Throat- "I speak"

6. The Third Eye- "I see"

7. The Crown- "I know"

I recommend the book, "Chakra Healing, A beginner's Guide to Self-Healing Techniques that Balance the Chakras," by Margarita Alcantara.

It has a wonderful section that has the Chakras

broken down with each one's main points of reference for growth.

**This song has an amazing visual available. If you watch the movie up to the end of this song, it shows what it felt like to me to realize that I have been limited in life by my societal education. My discovery that there is something supernatural in us all, made me voracious for more knowledge. I feel the NEED to know. I am determined to know. I am a human sponge who wants to awaken and live the life of beauty that is meant for each of us. This life of beauty is forever being stifled by our human lives. Until... we know!

*** This song was a catalyst for my husband so I had to add it. He came home during my awakening process and mentioned that it reminded him of how he feels about life and how he recognizes that he was letting fear and the grind tear him down and it is not going to do it anymore. He KNOWS that his negative thoughts were controlling him and his mood. It reminded him that he has things in his life to appreciate as well as things that need to change.

CHAPTER 16

Chakra 7

****
**

According to Dr. Dispenza, once we reach our highest state of consciousness, we should be able to change our focus by changing our emotions. I have interpreted that to mean that when you know what a happy and excited emotion feels like (like riding a roller coaster), you can pull that feeling up and it will change your current frequency to the frequency of that emotion. If you want to feel the whole warmth and love of our selves and our loved ones, we just think of it and we are in that frequency. This is why when you think good thoughts, your life starts to be more positive. It is an exercise of the mind. Even if we awaken, we have to keep practicing our meditation. Just like learning an instrument, learning math, learning to ride a bike, learning ANYTHING. Practice makes perfect.

If saying "meditating is important" sounds too "woo-woo" for some, maybe say something like, "Listen to your body. Let your mind listen to itself and let them listen to each other! BUT, to do that you need to resolve your issues and get them out of the way."

If we resolve our issues, there really should be nothing holding us back.

For example, the last "block" to my energy that I know that I cleared was my most amazing breakthrough. I let go of my hurt and trauma associated with the woman I relied on to be my mother and the neglect and abandonment from the man I relied on to be my father. I am now indifferent to them. They are just side characters in my life's story. Their combined characters dealt me a "trauma and abuse" card to help my soul grow in this game of life.

Knowing that, I am aware that I am no longer so tightly tethered to their lives. I have loosened all but the biological strings. I, in essence, unbraided their threads from the tapestry of my life. They are just the woman and man who gave me DNA. I am going to tell you...it is so freeing.

Funny how I am still interested in my ancestors and tracing their lineage. Why? Because they still made me! Plus, I love the search and putting the big puzzle together.

One night I was watching the Fifth Element (movie) I noticed that the images on the wall of the storage place of the stones had a similar look to finding your consciousness. Then I also noticed that before the planet could be saved, a mini sacrifice was given to each stone. Each one of the stones required a particular element.

Earth, Air, Fire, and Water.

Then the perfect human, the fifth element, couldn't reach her full consciousness until she could love. She was already perfect physically…. She could absorb information instantly so learning wasn't the issue. It was the emotion and acceptance of that feeling that they equated to "love."

Did that mean that her heart's energy was blocked?

It helps to remember that even though her

cells had all of her DNA and memories, she was what, three days old? Her new body had no reference for the emotion of love, until she could feel it in a reciprocal manner.

I think that the word "LOVE" is probably the most misunderstood word in the English language. It can be used as a substitute word for feelings that are just a fraction of the actual feeling.

Love is part of the key....to everything.

Until we see everything with that overwhelming feeling (love) radiating from out heart energy we can't ascend or awaken to our existence.

When this happens, there is no fear. NONE!!

My previous fears are gone for now! I know what it feels like to no longer be scared to face my mother. I have a new found inner peace and strength. I completely trust myself. Don't misunderstand. Fear is not the same thing as caution. I can still be cautious before I make any decision.

Actually, being cautious is our own

subconscious way to examine our environment
and circumstance. It should always be a step in
all of our thoughts. Even if it is in that quick
moment before we speak to someone and
hope to convey our message without harm.

CHAPTER 17

*!
*!

I have awakened! It is happening!

Dec 7, 2021!!!

I know that I am more than the 3D version of a human. I have had a truly transcendent moment.

I am in AWE!

This is how it happened for me...

I had taken a nice dose of a medically approved and natural "herb" for my swelling caused by my autoimmune disorder. I was lying next to my husband watching a particular Christmas movie and it hit me. I heard all of the voices. I felt ALL of the love. I had so many awe inspiring emotions. I talked to the beings that have been guiding me. I asked about some world events too.

It was all communicated to me through some of my favorite movie personalities.

Yes. It came through in a way that I can handle.

There were no lies, no bad feelings of ANY KIND!! And, MAN! I had so much laughter and nothing but happy tears.

The whole process of awakening didn't scare me. Why would something so beautiful scare you? And it is in EVERY one of us.

Believe it or not, mine came though as the voices and mental images of the cast of the movie, "Grown Ups!" Yes! Adam Sandler, Kevin James, and Maya Rudolf were the main speakers. Adam Sandler, especially!!

They told me that they thought that Grown Ups would be the movie to wake me up, but it turned out to be ELF! (I had watched Grown Ups before Elf). So "Buddy the Elf" came through, TOO! Not Will Ferrell, but a real person somewhere in my existence that somewhat mirrored him. We knew each other and he verified it in so many ways.

I asked why he told me a wrong name: "But your name is Buddy," to which he instantly proclaimed, "Bingo!"

It was unbelievable and amazing at the same time.

I laughed so hard at the words said and the personalities that were so present. I asked about so many things.

While I was crying and feeling overwhelmed, I slipped up and said, "Jesus Christ!" To which, an actual being in that form (to me) poked his head around a now present door frame (in my mind) and said, "Yes?"(in a silly way… like Yyyyyes?)

I was shocked. I asked if that was really him? They said that this being was indeed the man we know as "Jesus." (…. and thanks to a few more slip ups of "Jesus Christ!" and the same exact response that followed). I started giggling. I asked if that was why so many people tell you not to say his name in vain?

In unison, all of the "cast" loudly proclaimed, "YES!" It was one of those exasperated answers that you can almost see the eye rolls of aggravation. Oh MY GOD!! That is so damned funny!! (Yes, they don't care if you use the word "God," for some reason.) I will have to think about that.

Poor soul! But what a good hearted sport! He found a way to bring it to everyone's attention without being negative! I wouldn't expect anything less from the actual being that was Jesus in body.

How many times a day does he ("Jesus") poke his head around the corner and say, "YYyyyyyes?"

It is nice to know that there are still things that are aggravating...I mean humorous...to beings (the "cast") that are more evolved than me.

There is NO ill intent in their reactions. It may be a bit annoying, but it is completely accepted and loved by them all.

I learned a few things that were profound as well. Some were terrifying for the world and others were beautiful yet unrecognized by so many. I was one that was not aware.

My sweet pup, Winnie, is the physical

manifestation of my inner child. She is such a beautiful, sweet, sassy, obstinate, picky, smart and playful soul.

She is the very first pup that I have had this kind of connection with. I can now fully see why. I see her and I do cherish her. SO VERY MUCH! I have called her "my sweet baby," "my angel," and the like, and now I KNOW that she is the real thing.

I thought about the way she reacted to my sister, mother, and father, when they visited for my son's graduation. She didn't care for my sister. My sister annoyed her. When I was a child and my baby sister was little she DID annoy me!

My Winnie must have been reacting to her inner child. It brings me such joy to see this through new eyes. My Winnie did warm up to my sister. But, not until my sister backed off and allowed Winnie to decide if she wanted to know her. Plus, EXCUSE ME? She is the LITTLE sister! Isn't that funny?

Winnie did not like my dad, AT ALL! No explanation needed.

My Winnie nervously loved my mom. I had never seen this reaction from her. She almost seemed confused. She begged for her attention but was scared around her at the same time. She was almost to the point where she tinkles from too much feeling. It was so strange to watch. I didn't understand it at the time.

My inner child…that sweet baby just wanted my mom's love and attention. My mom tried to shoo her away a few times. She tried not to get annoyed at the unexpected love of an animal. It is not common to my mom.

My mom eventually gave her attention a time or two. Of course, Winnie just wanted more once she did. My mom would shoo her away immediately and say, "Okay, that's enough!" and walk away quickly or tuck her hands up high on her chest.

Wow. What a lesson right in front of my eyes.

Now I understand when people say that you can learn a lot about a person by the way they treat animals. Isn't that sad?

No, humans don't seem to deserve dogs. But, I am sure glad that they rocket through our lives when we need them. We can only aspire to be as pure hearted as a dog (or a cat, bunny, horse, etc...it didn't feel like it was exclusive to dogs!)

It definitely makes sense that the word "dog" is a tiny mirror image of GOD.

Once we figure out that we create our own world with our thoughts, creativity, sound, vibration and frequency, it makes sense when I have heard others say that we are our own GOD. How else would we be able to produce the manifestation of our inner child? It is a little supernatural/magical and sad at the same time.

It was also revealed to me that my other pup, Oliver, is the inner child of my oldest son that was badly hurt when he had a near death experience from what I hope was an accidental overdose.

That is an experience I hope to never have to see again, for anyone. I watched my son go from death to living in his subconscious world for two weeks to slowly coming back to having full mental capacity over the next month before being healed enough to be discharged from the hospital. Watching that from the outside is misery. It is life altering and eye opening.

When I realized that my baby had actually died, (or nicked a bit of his soul off...or however it is accomplished) to make this wonderful physical representation (Oliver) of his inner child, I cried.

I cried so hard. But MY OWN SON comforted me. His presence was there when I realized what had happened to his "soul." He must have known that I would need him in that moment. (I wonder if that is one of the places he went when he "died?")

In his sweet and beautiful voice, he said, "It's okay, Momma. It's okay." He was hugging me with his arm over my back and rubbing my back with his palm only, in the special way that he does. There was nothing but love and acceptance. Everyone just waited for me to be emotional with my son. They gave us privacy without leaving through it all.

Somebody said something funny and had me laughing soon after. It broke up the serious moment.

My husband started stirring, and one of the "cast" pointed out that they (and me) need to stop making so much noise before we wake up the hubby. Then they used some of my own words about him to describe him again.

("Yeah, wouldn't want to wake up 'Mr. Yumminess!" -Kevin James character)

… which made me laugh…

Then I said, "Well he's freakin hot!" They all said, in unison again, "We KNOW!"

(Besides, he is all of those things to me… and they know and find humor in it all.)

They all started tuning out.

Then, as the Adam Sandler character was leaving he hurriedly said, "One more thing… Want To Touch the Hiney! (in his old school character's voice). Goodnight!" and quickly closed the door (in my mind)

... I could not help but laugh.

I would have one of them pop in and out of my mind for a while. I am guessing to keep an eye on me to make sure I was handling the flood of information and that the many revelations were being handled with love and care.

I spent a couple of days processing the information and making sure that my human inclination to be negative or take a selfish path of thought is reverted to the actual love filled path I want to remain on.

****
**

Before I got to this point, I had signs that something was happening to me that I could not seem to make sense of, until now.

For weeks, I had those horrible dreams. So vivid. So real. They were other dimensions, other lives. I was so tired. Yet, wanted to have tons of sex. I had many emotional break throughs and continuously wanted to learn more to get my mind where I wanted.

My body was just achy and tired.

I figured out that it is my body transitioning out of survival mode and resetting itself to where it should be...in a complete state of balance. Factory reset... so to speak.

I have to give my body time. I am always hungry but even the thought of food makes my stomach turn, especially certain meats. Mushrooms seem to help.

My body is like a brand new baby bird that just fell out of the nest. My brain has to let my body rest, heal, and grow into the beautiful and colorful bird that is ready to fly and take its place in the sky!

Every energy point, every emotion faced, every trial (and error) in my life accepted, every (healthy) kink, every word spoken, every note sang, every good thought, and every bad...made me and my existence.

It ALL is my collection of knowledge to draw from to see and create my future. I see it in its true form.

To me, it looks like one of those fancy spirally

broccolis except it never stops multiplying and spiraling. That is how I see everyone's thoughts in 3D form, or as close as I can get. Our universe is another story all together. When I told my husband what I saw and heard, he was genuinely concerned that I had a psychotic break. (He is the sweetest and silliest sometimes.)

I will continue to meditate and stay in the positive. I will continue my hot bubble bath routine. I will continue to read my tarot cards, and use any means to keep my mind on the right track. It is actually just beginning for me. I was shown my purpose. If I want it to come true, I have a lot of work to do.

I also have to slow down when I talk to people. I am getting so much information from my higher self that it is flooding my brain and I am having a problem controlling my brain to mouth filter. When someone is telling me a story, I want to finish their story for them. Or I will try to comfort them in the middle of their story to help them heal and then that sends their story in the wrong direction.

I am a giver. I can't help it and it is a trait that

I want to keep.

The only hiccup for me in being a giver is that I want to give too much too fast. I am one of those people that can't keep a gift a secret from the recipient because I know it will make them happy.

The joy that is evident on their face and in their heart when I see their happiness makes being "a giver" something to be proud of.

I think that being proud of myself is just something that I need to get comfortable with.

This new me deserves it.

Update: On Christmas Eve of this past year (2021), I was shown some very important information about my childhood. I was shown when I began to feel unloved by my mom. It was a revelation that I never would have had, had I not awakened.

It started when I was a toddler. I formed a very deep and long lasting injury to my own heart. It wasn't her actions so much as her words. It was the misunderstanding of a toddler. It just never got dealt with properly.

I had a head injury from falling down the stairs while playing with my sister and the other kids in our apartment complex. We were using cardboard boxes as sleds and were sliding down from the second floor to the ground floor. Needless to say, I couldn't maintain my grip with my tiny toddler fingers. I tumbled and ended up with about 6 stitches.

When at the hospital, the doctor came into my room and said that he was going "to sew" me up.

This TERRIFIED me!

The only sewing I had ever seen was when my mom would sew at her sewing machine. My mom said that it was okay to "sew me up" to the doctor. My tiny toddler brain thought that she was giving the okay for them to smash my head so that it would fit under the needle. From this occurrence, my heart thought that my mom didn't love me and that she wanted me to hurt. I felt it deeply.

After, my strong will kicked in. I didn't want to do anything she said. I only wanted the approval of my dad.

It set off a series of events that just fueled more abuse. This caused mild traumatic brain injuries. I had the symptoms. I would try to adjust. Then as I healed, my anger, hate, and strong will would return. So then we would repeat the cycle.

That doesn't give an excuse or reason for the child abuse. She was still the one with all of the power in the dynamic.

This vicious cycle ended with me. Knowing this information just affirmed that choosing my mental health and happiness, by cutting ties with my parents, is the right move. I can not continue exposing my lightened soul to such darkness.

I am still growing and learning.

This is just the beginning.